ACADIA
THE COMPLETE GUIDE
3rd Edition

©2010 DESTINATION PRESS & ITS LICENSORS
ISBN: 978-09825172-0-8

Written & Photographed
by James Kaiser

This book would not have been possible without the help of many generous people. Special thanks to Wanda Moran, Ginny Reams, Brooke Childrey, and the entire staff at Acadia National Park, professors Bill Carpenter and Helen Hess at COA, Mindy Viechnicki at Allied Whale, Rebecca Cole-Will at the Abbe Museum, and Erika Latty at Unity College. Special thanks also to Andrea Rincon, Rick Crowe, Whitney Crowe, Kevin Crowe, and every other Crowe, Steve Foley, Cathy McDonald, Dan Shubert, Scott Petticord, Abby Johnston, Matt Tracy, Alyssa and Seth, Josia and Maria.

As always, a very special thanks to my family & friends, who have always supported me. Even when they shouldn't have.

All information in this guide has been exhaustively researched, but names, phone numbers, and other details do change. If you encounter a change or mistake while using this guide, please send an email to changes@jameskaiser.com. Your input will help improve future editions of this guide.

Legal Disclaimer:

Additional Photography & Image Credits
National Park Service: 104, 105, 109, 124, 129; Bangor Daily News: 130
Bar Harbor Historical Society: 122, 126, 127; Kim Strauss: page 31; USGS: page 69
North Wind Picture Archives: 75, 76, 112, 120, 123; Hinckley Company: 260
Eyewire: page 85, 97, 100, 101; Corel: page 84, 98, 102; Getty: page 88, 96
Allied Whale: 117; iStockphoto: page 89, 90, 91, 92, 93, 94, 95, 99, 101
Printed in Thailand

ACADIA

• THE COMPLETE GUIDE •

3rd Edition

JAMES KAISER

CONGRATULATIONS!

IF YOU'VE PURCHASED this book, you're going to Mount Desert Island. Perhaps you're already here. If so, you're in one of the most amazing places in the world—a gorgeous island filled with granite mountains that tower above the sea. An island so beautiful that nearly 40% of it has been permanently protected as Acadia National Park. A place where you can hike in the morning, sea kayak in the afternoon, and sit down to a gourmet meal at night.

So who am I and why should you listen to me? My name is James Kaiser, and I was born and raised near Mount Desert Island. I spent my childhood summers hiking and biking in Acadia National Park, and my college summers working in Bar Harbor. Although my work as a travel writer and photographer has carried me away from Mount Desert Island, I return as often as possible. It's my favorite place in the world. I know the park, I know the towns, I know the locals—I know the secrets! And I'm going to show you the best that Mount Desert Island has to offer.

You could easily spend a month exploring Mount Desert Island and not run out of things to do. But if you're like most people, you've only got a few days. Make those few days count! With a limited amount of time, you've got to plan your trip wisely. This book puts the best of Mount Desert Island and Acadia National Park at your fingertips, helping you maximize your time for an unforgettable vacation. Whether you're here to hike, here to sight-see, or just here to eat and hang out, *Acadia: The Complete Guide* is the only guide you'll need.

Now let me show you the best that Mount Desert Island and Acadia National Park have to offer!

CONTENTS

ADVENTURES (21–31)

Hiking, biking, sea kayaking, rock climbing, sailing—Mount Desert Island has it all. The only question is what not to do!

BASICS (32–51)

Everything you need to know, from seasonal weather patterns and local transportation, to the island's best lobster and beer.

GEOLOGY (52–57)

Over the past 500 million years, Acadia has been home to colliding continents, erupting volcanoes, massive glaciers and countless other splendid catastrophes.

ECOLOGY & WILDLIFE (58–103)

Lying at the boundary of two major ecological zones, Mount Desert Island is home to a stunning range of plants and animals. And the pristine waters offshore are filled with fascinating creatures, from starfish to seals to humpback whales.

HISTORY (104–133)

Learn about Mount Desert Island's fascinating history. Originally home to Wabanaki Indians, the island was settled by whites in the late 1700s. Famous artists arrived in the mid-1800s, and within a few decades Bar Harbor was one of the most exclusive resorts in America. In 1919 wealthy summer visitors spearheaded the creation of Acadia National Park—the first national park east of the Mississippi.

ACADIA NATIONAL PARK (134-221)

Nearly half of Mount Desert Island has been protected as Acadia National Park. The Park Loop Road is Acadia's most popular attraction, but the park's hiking trails and carriage roads are truly world-class. Acadia also includes Schoodic Peninsula, on the mainland, and half of Isle au Haut, a small, rugged island 15 miles to the southwest.

ISLAND TOWNS (222–267)

From bustling tourist towns to traditional fishing villages, there's something for everyone here. The eastern half of the island is home to Bar Harbor, the island's unofficial capital, and the exclusive summer colonies of Northeast Harbor and Seal Harbor. The western "quiet" side of the island sees far fewer tourists, but it's home to some of the island's best attractions.

OFFSHORE ISLANDS (268–285)

Over a dozen smaller islands are found in the waters off Mount Desert Island, and several of them are accessible by ferry. Day tripping to a small island with a year-round fishing community is a fascinating experience. Physically cut off from the mainland, these islands are home to some of the most rugged and remote communities in America.

HIGHLIGHTS

Hiking (p.21)

Acadia National Park is home to some of the best coastal hiking in America with over 100 miles of trails crisscrossing the park. From easy strolls to nearly vertical climbs, there's something for everyone here.

Carriage Roads (p.199)

Summer resident John D. Rockefeller, Jr. built over 40 miles of carriage roads on his private property, then donated the roads to the park. Today the carriage roads and their 17 exquisite stone bridges are perfect for biking, horseback riding, or horse-drawn carriage rides.

Bass Harbor Lighthouse (p.266)

Perched on the jagged rocks at the southern tip of Mount Desert Island, Bass Harbor Lighthouse, built in 1858, is one of the most beautiful lighthouses in Maine.

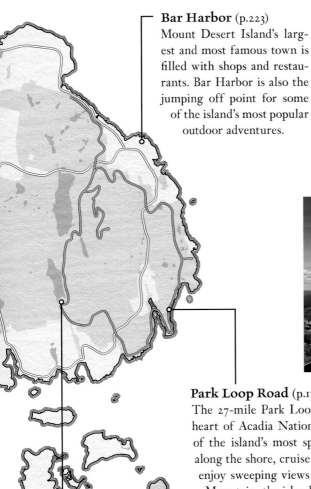

Bar Harbor (p.223)

Mount Desert Island's largest and most famous town is filled with shops and restaurants. Bar Harbor is also the jumping off point for some of the island's most popular outdoor adventures.

Park Loop Road (p.137)

The 27-mile Park Loop Road cuts through the heart of Acadia National Park and passes some of the island's most spectacular scenery. Drive along the shore, cruise through lush forests, and enjoy sweeping views from the top of Cadillac Mountain, the island's highest peak.

Jordan Pond House (p.166)

Popovers and tea at the Jordan Pond House have been a tradition on Mount Desert Island for over 100 years. The only thing better than oven-fresh popovers are the amazing views from the shore of Jordan Pond.

INTRODUCTION

TWO-THIRDS OF the way up the craggy coast of Maine lies Mount Desert Island, home to granite mountains, picturesque harbors, and Acadia National Park. Mount Desert Island is the crown jewel of coastal New England—the only place on the East Coast where the mountains literally meet the sea. Those mountains, rounded and smoothed by Ice Age glaciers, form one of the most distinctive profiles in the world. From the sea they look like a string of giant ice cream scoops rising up out of the water. Cadillac Mountain, the island's tallest peak, is 1,530 feet—the highest point on the eastern seaboard north of Rio de Janeiro.

Nestled between the island's 24 mountain peaks are forests, lakes, meadows, marshes and the only fjord on the East Coast: Somes Sound, which nearly cuts the island in two. Roughly two-thirds of Mount Desert Island has been set aside as Acadia National Park. At just 46,000 acres, Acadia is one of the smallest national parks in America. But it's also one of the most popular, luring roughly 3 million visitors a year. Acadia's most famous attraction is the Park Loop Road, which runs along the island's rugged eastern shore before cutting through the forest, passing by two pristine lakes, then twisting and turning to the top of Cadillac Mountain.

Acadia also boasts 125 miles of stunning hiking trails and 45 miles of carriage roads perfect for biking or horseback riding. In addition to land on Mount Desert Island, the park also includes Schoodic Peninsula, on the mainland, and half of Isle au Haut, a remote, rugged island 14 miles southwest of Mount Desert Island.

About half a dozen coastal villages dot the shores of Mount Desert Island—some, like Bar Harbor, built around tourism; others, like Bass Harbor, carrying on as quiet fishing hamlets, much as they always have. There are also wealthy summer towns like Seal Harbor and Northeast Harbor, and historic villages like Somesville, the island's oldest town. Several offshore islands are also accessible by ferry, making them great for day tripping.

In the days before Columbus, Mount Desert Island was the seasonal home of the Wabanaki Indians. Hardy coastal settlers arrived in the late 1700s, followed by artists and tourists several decades later. By the late 1800s, the island was one of the most exclusive summer resorts in America, but by the 1930s the glamour of the island had started to fade. In 1947 a massive fire burned down many of the island's once grand mansions. Following the fire, the island rebuilt and reestablished itself as a major tourist mecca. Today it attracts a diverse mix of summer visitors: outdoor junkies, fanny-packed retirees, college students, hippies and billionaires—proving there's something for everyone here.

Physically beautiful, ecologically impressive, and culturally unique, Mount Desert Island is one of the most fascinating islands in the world.

Cranberry Isles & Mount Desert Island

Champlain Mountain

Bass Harbor

Bear Island Lighthouse

Acadia Mountain

HIKING

Acadia NATIONAL PARK is a day hiker's paradise. There are over two dozen peaks on Mount Desert Island, and nearly all of them are accessible via an extensive network of hiking trails maintained by the park. All told, there are over 100 miles of hiking trails in Acadia, ranging from gentle strolls through spruce-pine forest to sheer ascents up nearly vertical cliffs. And when it comes to dramatic coastal views, few hiking destinations in America can compare with Acadia.

Even if Acadia's trails were just crumbling dirt paths, they'd still be amazing. But here on Mount Desert Island, home to hundreds of rich, civic-minded summer residents, the trails have been spruced up beyond belief. In 1999 the non-profit Friends of Acadia and Acadia National Park launched *Acadia Trails Forever*, a $13 million project that fully restored the entire trail system. The result? Today Acadia's trails are in the best shape they've been in years. Nearly every trail is well-marked with cairns (small stone piles) and blue blazes painted onto trees and rocks. Many trails feature hand-carved stone steps that gracefully lead you up otherwise challenging terrain. This is rich man's hiking, open to all. If you visit Mount Desert Island without going on at least one hike, you should return to the mainland ashamed.

This book provides maps and trail info for eight amazing hikes (see pages 182–196). And while it's hard to play favorites, if I had to pick my top three, I'd go with The Precipice, Acadia Mountain, and Penobscot Mountain. All of the hikes listed on pages 182–196 are rated moderate, strenuous, or ladder (strenuous with some climbing on iron ladders or rungs). If you're looking for easy hikes, check out The Shorepath or Bar Island in Bar Harbor (p.225), Thuya Lodge in Northeast Harbor (p.245), or Ship Harbor and Wonderland in Bass Harbor (p.265). And if your thirst for hiking exceeds that of the average visitor, pick up a copy of Tom St. Germain's *A Walk In The Park,* available at stores throughout the island.

Also note that the Island Explorer shuttle system (p.34) is a fantastic resource for hikers. By removing the hassle of parking, the Island Explorer opens up new realms of hiking possibilities. In the pre-Island Explorer days, you had to loop back to wherever you parked your car. Now you can take full advantage of Acadia's extensive network of trails, starting in one place and finishing someplace totally different. Long live the Island Explorer!

Hiking Rules: Overnight backpacking is not allowed in Acadia National Park. Bicycles and horses are not allowed on any hiking trails. All pets must be kept on a leash no greater than six feet in length at all times. Swimming is prohibited in lakes or ponds that are posted as public water supplies.

Porcupine Islands

SEA KAYAKING

THE CRAGGY, 3,000-MILE long coast of Maine is one of the country's top sea kayaking destinations. And everything sea kayakers love about Maine—pine-covered islands, calm bays dotted with colorful lobster buoys, and pristine waters filled with seals and harbor porpoises—can be found around Mount Desert Island. With the scenery, the wildlife, and the joy of paddling, it's no wonder that sea kayaking is one of Mount Desert Island's most popular activities.

That said, the waters around Mount Desert Island do present some unique challenges. Cold water, craggy shorelines, fishing boats, dense fog, unpredictable weather, 12-foot tides, and swift currents are just a few of the challenges you might encounter. With a trained guide, you're in safe hands. Without a trained guide, you can get in trouble fast. Fortunately, Mount Desert Island is home to some of the best sea kayak guides in Maine, so everyone, even absolute beginners, can get in on the action. The following outfitters specialize exclusively on sea kayaking, and rates generally run between $35 and $50 for a 2–4 hour tour.

AQUATERRA ADVENTURES
This highly recommended outfitter specializes in trips around the Porcupine Islands and Frenchman Bay. Their convenient location launches directly from the Bar Harbor Pier, and they offer a Family Discovery Trip specifically tailored to young children.
(One West Street, 207-288-0007, www.aquaterra-adventures.com)

NATIONAL PARK SEA KAYAKING
This eco-oriented outfitter focuses exclusively on tours on the quiet western shores of Mount Desert Island, which is calmer than Frenchman Bay and offers terrific wildlife viewing opportunities. They also offer overnight expeditions with camping on remote offshore islands.
(39 Cottage Street, 207-288-0342, www.acadiakayak.com)

MAINE STATE SEA KAYAK
Based in Southwest Harbor, this is the sister company of National Park Sea Kayaking. They also specialize in eco-tours of the quiet, western side of Mount Desert Island.
(254 Main Street, 207-244-9500, www.mainestateseakayak.com)

Carriage Roads

BIKING

$^?/_D$

IF YOU LOVE biking, there's plenty to love about Acadia National Park. Although the park's mountains and hiking trails are off-limits to mountain bikers, there are plenty of on-road options in and around the park, including paved roads that skirt the coastline and gravel roads that explore the island's forests.

The most famous biking on Mount Desert Island is on Acadia's carriage roads. This 57-mile network of gravel roads, built by John D. Rockefeller, Jr. between 1913 and 1940, was originally designed for horse-drawn carriages. Today there are few horse-drawn carriages on the carriage roads, but the gravel roads are perfect for mountain bikes. The carriage road system stretches from Bar Harbor to Seal Harbor, meandering through beautiful forests, passing over a dozen lakes and ponds, and crossing a series of 17 dramatic stone bridges. The overall experience feels like something out of a fairy tale. Not surprisingly, the carriage roads are one of Acadia's top attractions.

Most of the carriage roads follow a relatively gentle grade—they were designed with the relaxation of carriage riders in mind—but there are some hilly sections throughout the system that offer a good workout. Maps and other info on the carriage roads can be found on pages 199–207. The best entry points for the Carriage Roads near Bar Harbor are Eagle Lake and Duck Brook Bridge. From late June through September, the popular Bicycle Express shuttle runs every 30 minutes between the Bar Harbor Village Green and Eagle Lake. Farther south, you can hop on the carriage roads at Bubble Pond, the Jordan Pond House, or at one of two stops along Route 198 north of Northeast Harbor.

If you're more interested in cycling on paved roads, you can check out the famous 27-mile Park Loop Road (p.137), which passes by some of Acadia's top attractions. During the busy summer months, however, you'll have to contend with traffic, tour buses and plenty of gawking tourists. A more relaxing biking experience is found on the quiet western side of the island, particularly Route 102A and Route 102 between Bass Harbor and Pretty Marsh.

There are also some great off-island cycling options. The six-mile loop road on Schoodic Peninsula (p.209) sees far fewer tourists than the Park Loop Road, and it's accessible via a ferry from Bar Harbor. There's also great biking on Swan's Island (p.279), a 7,000-acre island six miles south of Mount Desert Island that's accessible via a ferry from Bass Harbor. Swan's Island has over a dozen miles of paved roads that pass by working harbors and quaint fishing villages. And because Swan's Island only has about 350 year-round residents, there's little traffic.

Bicycle rentals are available in Bar Harbor (p.232) and SW Harbor (p.258).

Otter Cliffs

ROCK CLIMBING

ACADIA'S BOLD MOUNTAINS and stunning coastal scenery make it one of the most unique climbing destinations on the East Coast. There's lots of great rock climbing from Georgia to Maine, but only in Acadia can you scale sheer cliffs rising directly out of the ocean. Spend a day climbing above crashing waves while sailboats and lobsterboats pass by offshore, and you'll understand why thousands of climbers flock to Acadia in the summer and fall.

If you've never climbed before, Acadia is a great place to learn. There are plenty of beginner climbs, and two outfitters in Bar Harbor offer private lessons and guided climbs. Rates at both outfitters are similar. Private lessons run about $140 per half day, $250 per full day (including gear and transportation). Both outfitters also offer discounts if you sign up as part of a group. If you're an experienced rock climber, be sure to pick up a copy of *Acadia: A Climber's Guide*, by Jeff Butterfield.

The most famous and popular climbing spot on the island is Otter Cliffs (p.160). These vertical cliffs rise straight out of the ocean, offering stunning views of the rocky shore along Ocean Drive in Acadia National Park. Climbs at Otter Cliffs range in difficulty from 5.4 to 5.12. Due to its fame, popularity, and accessibility, Otter Cliffs is often crowded in the summer months. But there are plenty of other climbs on the island that offer equally stunning views and few, if any, crowds. South Wall, a multi-pitch climb on Champlain Mountain, rises hundreds of feet above sea level and offers terrific views of Frenchman Bay. There are also some challenging climbs on Great Head (next to Sand Beach) and on South Bubble at the north end of Jordan Pond.

Note: be extremely careful at seaside climbs. The Gulf of Maine's high tides, icy water, and strong current can be lethal. In 2004 a climber at Otter Cliffs accidentally dropped his shoe in the ocean and jumped into the water to get it. But the waves tossed him against the rocks, knocking him unconscious, and he drowned.

ACADIA MOUNTAIN GUIDES
Based out of Alpenglow Adventure Sports on 198 Main Street, AMG offers a wide range of climbing lessons and a well-stocked retail store.
(207-288-8186, www.acadiamountainguides.com)

ATLANTIC CLIMBING SCHOOL
ACS, the oldest climbing school on the island, offers everything from pure beginner courses to guiding and advanced skills.
(207-288-2521, www.climbacadia.com)

Sailing on the Alice. E

SAILING & BOAT TRIPS

THE BEAUTIFUL, ISLAND-STREWN coast of Maine is one of America's premier boating destinations, and the waters around Mount Desert Island offer some of the best boating in Maine. Fortunately, you don't need to own a boat or know anything about boating to enjoy some time on the water. There are over a dozen boat tours departing from Mount Desert Island, offering everything from mellow day sails to whale watches on jet-powered catamarans.

I have to confess, I love boats. I've never been on a boat trip here that I didn't enjoy—if nothing else for the stunning views of Mount Desert Island from the water. That said, some boat trips are definitely better than others. Listed on the following pages are my favorite boat trips. If none of those trips strikes your fancy, there are plenty of others that depart from Bar Harbor (p.230), Northeast Harbor (p.246), and Southwest Harbor (p.258).

The most popular boat trips are motorboat trips, which cover more distance in less time than sailboat trips. The wide variety of motorboat trips includes whale watching, nature tours, lobstering demonstrations, deep sea fishing, lighthouse tours and day trips to small, offshore islands.

Sailboat trips are a great way to spend a relaxing day on the water. These trips tend to focus more on the sailing experience and the scenery than any one specific activity. The main question with sailboats is: big or small? Small sailboats offer a more intimate experience where you'll definitely get to know your captain and fellow passengers. Most of the small sailboat operators are also happy to offer private charters if you're willing to pay extra. Some even offer sunset sails, lobster bakes, and overnight trips.

At the other end of the spectrum are big sailboats, which offer a smoother ride, a better value, and the unique experience of watching crew members hoist massive sails to catch the wind—a rare sight these days, but one that was a vital part of daily life in coastal Maine for hundreds of years. The only downside to a big sailboat is the cattle-call feeling that comes when you're one of dozens of passengers.

Finally, if you're *really* into boating, head to Southwest Harbor (the unofficial boat capital of the island), where you can rent boats (p.258) or buy them (p.261).

ACADIA'S BEST BOAT TRIPS

Starfish Enterprise (51 feet)

I can't recommend this "Dive-In Theater" trip highly enough! The supremely entertaining Diver Ed (Maine's version of the Croc Hunter) and his knowledgeable wife "Captain Evil" show visitors Maine's fascinating underwater world from the 51-foot *Starfish Enterprise*. After putting on a dry suit, Diver Ed jumps overboard with an HD video camera and seeks out strange and interesting creatures on the seafloor. The live images are then projected onboard, showing crabs, starfish, lobsters, and other critters living in their natural habitat. Ed then resurfaces with the animals for a highly entertaining show-and-tell. The cliché "Fun for the whole family" certainly applies here. If you're visiting with kids, this will probably be the highlight of their trip. $35 adults, $30 seniors, $25 children, $10 children under 4. (207-288-3483, www.divered.com)

Friendship V (112 feet)

This jet-powered, 112-foot aluminum catamaran whisks passengers 25-30 miles off the coast of Mount Desert Island where sightings of humpback, finback, and minke whales are common. The Gulf of Maine is one of the world's premier whale habitats, and the sight of these gentle giants in the wild is always breathtaking. You'll also be treated to stunning offshore views of Mount Desert Island and potential porpoise, seal, and seabird sightings. I like the morning trip, which combines whale watching with a trip to Petit Manan Island, a small offshore island home to puffins and other seabirds, as well as Maine's second tallest lighthouse. Closely affiliated with Allied Whale (p.79), a trip on the Friendship V is enjoyable *and* helps a great cause. (207-288-2386, www.barharborwhales.com).

R.L. Gott (40 feet)

For nearly two decades Captain Kim Strauss has been offering fantastic narrated cruises through the gorgeous islands just south of Bass Harbor. If you're interested in wildlife, coastal Maine history, lobstering culture or idyllic island scenery, this tour can't be beat. Captain Strauss has been plying the waters of Blue Hill Bay since he was two months old, and he's a wealth of fascinating local info. Two trips are offered: a 3.5-hour lunch cruise that includes a stop on Frenchboro (an offshore island with a small fishing community) and a two-hour afternoon trip focused on wildlife.
(207-244-5785, www.bassharborcruises.com)

Margaret Todd (151 feet)

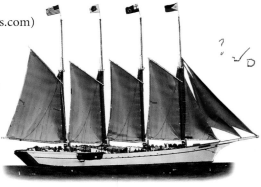

This large, elegant schooner—the only four-masted schooner to work New England's waters in over 50 years—offers two-hour cruises around Frenchman Bay and the Porcupine Islands. The Margaret Todd sails three times daily (10 am, 2 pm, sunset) with all trips departing from the Bar Harbor Inn pier. Tickets are available on the pier. Adults: $35, children $25.
(207-288-4585 , www.downeastwindjammer.com)

Alice E. (42 feet)

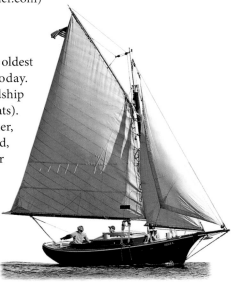

This gorgeous sailboat, built in 1899, is the oldest known Friendship Sloop still sailing today. (In the days before diesel engines, Friendship Sloops were the original Maine lobsterboats). The *Alice E.*'s affable captain, Karl Brunner, had this historic vessel exquisitely restored, and today it sails from Southwest Harbor on trips around Somes Sound and the Cranberry Isles—arguably the two most scenic waterways in the region. Two-hour sails are $50 per passenger, and reservations are required.
(207-266-5210, www.sailacadia.com)

Mount Desert Island
BASICS

Getting to Mount Desert Island

The good news is that you don't need a boat to get to Mount Desert Island, which is only an island by about 50 feet at low tide. A small bridge connects the island to the mainland via Route 1A. How you get to that bridge is up to you.

BY CAR

Driving your own car is the most popular way to get to Mount Desert Island. From southern Maine there are two options: the fast route and the scenic route. The fast route follows I-95 north to Bangor, heads east on I-395 to Route 1A, and follows Route 1A to Mount Desert Island (about a 3–4 hour drive from the Maine/New Hampshire border). The scenic route starts in Portland and follows Route 1 up the coast of Maine to Ellsworth. From there you'll connect with Route 1A to Mount Desert Island. Between Portland and Ellsworth, you'll pass through Rockland, Camden, and several other gorgeous coastal towns. The scenic route takes about 5–6 hours from Portland (not counting weekend traffic).

BY PLANE

The Hancock County/Bar Harbor Airport (www.bhbairport.com) is located in the town of Trenton on the mainland, 12 miles from downtown Bar Harbor. In the summer US Airways runs daily flights between Boston and Bar Harbor. The Island Explorer (p.34) runs free shuttles between the Bar Harbor Airport and downtown Bar Harbor from late June through August. Taxis and rental cars are also available year-round. The next closest airports are Bangor International Airport (located in Bangor, Maine, about a 1.5 hour drive from Mount Desert Island) and Portland International Jetport (located in Portland, Maine, about a 3.5 hour drive from Mount Desert Island).

BY BUS

Vermont Transit offers daily bus service to Bar Harbor from Portland and Bangor (800-552-8737, www.vermonttransit.com).

BY BOAT

Although you don't need a boat to get to Mount Desert Island, that option is certainly available. The high speed ferry *The Cat* (www.catferry.com) runs trips between Bar Harbor and Yarmouth, Nova Scotia. In addition, numerous cruise lines offer trips that call to port in Bar Harbor.

MOUNT DESERT ISLAND
At a Glance

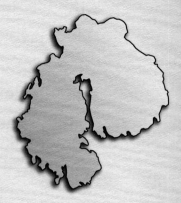

Area: 108 square miles

Length: 16 miles

Width: 10 miles

Mountain Peaks: 26

Lakes and Ponds: 28

Average Tides: 8–12 feet

Population: 10,500

Year-round Residences: 5,000

Summer Residences: 2,100

Avg. Annual Rainfall: 48 inches

Avg. Annual Snowfall: 61 inches

Total Assessed Value of Private Property on MDI: $4.6 Billion

Latitude: 44.3° N, Longitude: 68.3° W

If you headed due east from MDI you'd hit Bordeaux, France;
Bologna, Italy; the Gobi Desert, China; and Mongolia.

If you headed due south of MDI you'd hit Caracas, Venezuela;
La Paz, Bolivia; and Mendoza, Argentina.

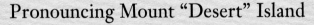

Pronouncing Mount "Desert" Island

Is the Desert in Mount Desert Island pronounced "desert" (as in the Sahara) or "dessert" (as in ice cream)? Strangely, Mainers say both, and the island's linguist roots offer little clarification. The island was named in 1604 by the French explorer Samuel Champlain, who dubbed it *L'Isle des Monts-déserts* ("Island of Barren Mountains"). The "desert" (Sahara) camp claims they are justified by the "Barren" description. The granite peaks, they argue, are void of vegetation, much like a desert. Meanwhile, the "dessert" (Ice Cream) camp claims the French pronunciation of *desert* sounds more like "dessert." In addition, Champlain was saying the peaks were "deserted" which sounds more like "dessert." Where do I fall? I grew up saying "dessert," a trait I learned from my mother (a 5th generation Mainer). And far be it for me to argue with mom.

Getting Around Mount Desert Island

BY CAR

Driving around Mount Desert Island is easy. There are only a handful of major roads, there are gas stations in every town, and because you're on an island, it's nearly impossible to get completely lost. The only hassle is parking, which is often in short supply in July and August, especially on the Park Loop Road.

ISLAND EXPLORER SHUTTLE

The best way to get around the island these days is the free Island Explorer Shuttle. These propane-powered buses were experimentally introduced in 1999 to reduce traffic and air pollution—and the experiment was wildly successful. Today the Island Explorer runs seven routes linking hotels, inns and campgrounds with popular destinations throughout the island. (An eighth shuttle route circles Schoodic Peninsula on the mainland.) Shuttles run from late June through mid-October, but service is scaled back after Labor Day. Island Explorer maps and timetables are available at any visitor center and on the Island Explorer Web site (www.exploreacadia.com). In addition to helping the environment, riding the Island Explorer completely removes the hassle of parking. So unless you're going somewhere the Island Explorer doesn't go (the top of Cadillac Mountain, for example), it's often easier and more convenient to take the Island Explorer.

TAXI COMPANIES

Acadia Cab (207-288-8294)

At Your Service Taxi (207-288-9222)

MDI Taxi & Touring Company (207-288-3333)

Visitor Information

THOMPSON ISLAND VISITOR CENTER

This small visitor center, located on tiny Thompson Island near the northern tip of MDI, is a great place to ask questions, pick up free publications, and inquire about last-minute lodging. Open 8am–6pm, mid-May to mid-October.

HULLS COVE VISITOR CENTER

Acadia National Park's main visitor center is also the start of the Park Loop Road and a minor hub for the Island Explorer. See page 138 for more info.

ACADIA INFORMATION CENTER

This information center on Route 3 in Trenton offers free brochures, interactive displays, and a knowledgeable staff. (800-358-8550, www.acadiainfo.com).

CHAMBERS OF COMMERCE

The island's local chambers of commerce are great in-town resources for basic questions, free brochures and publications, and last minute lodging options.

Bar Harbor Chamber of Commerce
(93 Cottage Street, Bar Harbor, 207-288-5103, www.barharborinfo.com)

Southwest Harbor/Tremont Chamber of Commerce
(204 Main Street, Southwest Harbor, 207-244-9264, www.acadiachamber.com)

Hotels & Lodging

There are dozens of places to stay on Mount Desert Island, and listing them all here would take dozens of pages. Rather than waste all that paper (when all you need is one room), I've posted all lodging information at www.jameskaiser.com.

Suffice to say, the vast majority of lodging is found in Bar Harbor, though Northeast Harbor and Southwest Harbor also have some great options. No matter where you end up, though, the island is small enough that you'll never be too far from anything. And if you find room prices on the island prohibitively expensive, try looking in off-island towns such as Trenton or Ellsworth.

Camping

Acadia National Park runs two campgrounds on Mount Desert Island: Blackwoods and Seawall. Both are situated in the forest with no ocean views, but both are just a short walk from the ocean. Each campground has a maximum capacity of six people per site. There are also about a dozen private campgrounds located outside the park (visit www.jameskaiser.com for private campground info). Acadia National Park also operates Duck Harbor Campground on far-flung Isle au Haut (p.219).

BLACKWOODS

Blackwoods Campground is located off Route 3 between Bar Harbor and Seal Harbor on the eastern side of Mount Desert Island. Because it's close to many of the Acadia's top attractions, it's Acadia's most popular campground. Reservations are required between June 15 and September 15. 300+ sites. Cost: $20 per night, April–November (877-444-6777, www.recreation.gov).

SEAWALL

This first-come, first-served campground is located near the southwestern tip of Mount Desert Island. Some people love the quiet, remote location; others find it a bit too far away from the island's top attractions (most of which are on the eastern half of the island). To snag a site in mid-summer, arrive at 8:30am when the ranger station opens. Open Memorial Day Weekend through September. 200 sites. Cost: $20 per night.

Weather & When to Go

Let me introduce you to Maine's most tired cliché: "If you don't like the weather, wait a minute. It'll change." But like all tired clichés, it's tired because it's true. The weather in Maine, especially along the coast, is highly unpredictable. It varies from day to day, month to month, and year to year. There's simply no rhyme or reason to it—as any local weatherman will attest. (Tough job, Maine weatherman.)

My favorite source of forecasts and weather info is the National Weather Service (www.nws.noaa.gov). But in my experience, even their forecasts are only partially reliable. Most are based on regional forecasts, and there's a tremendous amount of variability in the region. In my highly non-scientific study of local forecasts, I've found that 24-hour reports are right about 70% of the time, 48-hour reports are right about 50% of the time, 36-hour reports are right about 30% of the time, and any report over 36 hours is completely useless.

That said, when the weather's good, it's incredible—sunny, warm, with a cool ocean breeze. And even when it's bad—foggy, rainy, snowy—the coast has a beautiful mystique. Also keep in mind that, in terms of annual precipitation, coastal Maine is ranked second in America only to the Pacific Northwest. It can rain at any time of the year on short notice, so pack accordingly.

SPRING

Spring (aka Mud Season) definitely has its pros and cons. Melting ice and snow keep things soggy in the early spring, but by late spring the island has often dried out and temperatures can be divine. Spring is also bug season. Biting bugs are most active between mid-May and mid-June when running water provides optimum breeding conditions. But bug numbers depend considerably on how rainy it has been (see page 45 for more info on biting bugs). Spring is also when local businesses come out of their long winter hibernation. Hotels and shops start opening in late April, and by Memorial Day most of the island is open for business. But the peak tourist season doesn't officially kick into high gear until the Fourth of July, at which point everything is open.

SUMMER

Sunny summer days bring perfect temperatures to Mount Desert Island: high 70s with a cool ocean breeze. But summer can also bring thick fog that blankets the island for hours or sometimes days. Sunny or not, July is when things get busy on Mount Desert Island—booked hotels, waiting lists at restaurants, crowded parking lots, you name it. (This is all relative, of course. By Maine standards it's crazy, but New Yorkers will probably appreciate the peace and quiet.) August is even busier than July, with families trying to cram in one last vacation before school starts, and Mainers trying to enjoy one last blast of summer heat before fall. Then, just when things seem like they can't get any crazier, Labor Day hits and the peak season ends with a bang.

FALL

Fall is one of the best times to visit Mount Desert Island. The weather is crisp, the crowds are light, and the foliage is often spectacular. Weather in early September is generally divine, but temperatures always start dropping by the end of the month. Fall is also the busiest season for cruise ships, which dock in Bar Harbor and disgorge thousands of passengers onto the town's narrow streets. Still, there's always a dramatic lull in visitation in mid-September between peak summer season and "leaf peeping" season. Fall foliage generally peaks between October 13–22, but the dates can vary from year to year. (Check out www.mainefoliage.com for current conditions) By late October temperatures start dropping, tourists start departing en masse, and locals start hunkering down. By early November, many storefront windows in Bar Harbor are covered in plywood, and the island goes into hibernation for the winter.

WINTER

Winter is a cold, desolate season on Mount Desert Island. New England has some of the longest and most ferocious winters in the United States, and though the ocean warms things up a bit on the coast, that's not saying much. The average snowfall on Mount Desert Island is 61 inches, but the snow that falls often melts quickly, so it's of little use for winter sports. When the snow does stick, Acadia's carriage roads are great for cross country skiing, and the Park Loop Road is great for snowmobiling. But most hotels, restaurants, museums, and other attractions are closed for the season. There are, however, a few hardy restaurants and hotels that stay open year-round.

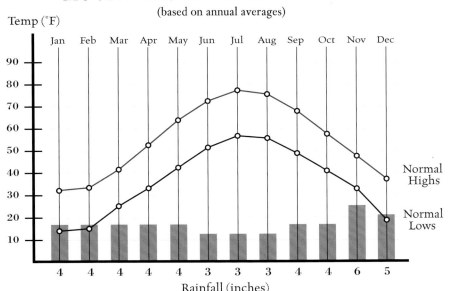

MOUNT DESERT ISLAND CLIMATE
(based on annual averages)

COASTAL MAINE WEATHER

Weather in coastal Maine is, in a word, unpredictable. Although summers on the coast are generally sunny and divine, conditions can change in an instant. What started out as a sunny day can end in rain, fog, or (in very rare cases) snow! It turns out that weather patterns in Maine—and all of New England for that matter—are more variable and more extreme than almost any other place the United States. As Mark Twain once said, "I reverently believe that the Maker who made us all makes everything in New England but the weather. I don't know who makes that, but I think it must be some raw apprentices in the weather-clerk's factory."

Maine is located at roughly 45° N latitude, exactly halfway between the equator and the North Pole. This puts Maine in the middle battleground between the hot, humid air of the tropics and the cold, dry air of the arctic. Storms in these middle latitudes follow fairly predictable paths called storm tracks, and almost all storm tracks in the United States have the potential to pass through Maine.

In addition to regular storms, Maine must also contend with hurricane season, which officially runs from June through November. Most hurricanes make landfall in the Southeast and dissipate long before reaching Maine. Those hurricanes that do make it to Maine generally arrive in August, September, or October, and most are Category 2 or less by the time they arrive.

Temperatures in Maine can vary dramatically throughout the year, but temperatures along the coast are moderated by the ocean. During the dog days of summer, when inland Maine is hot and humid, the Gulf of Maine's cold water keeps temperatures mild. And in the dead of winter, when inland Maine often suffers from sub-zero temperatures, the ocean's relative warmth boosts temperatures on the coast.

Long-term weather trends in Maine are influenced by a weather system known as the North Atlantic Oscillation (NAO). The NAO results from the interaction between a semi-permanent low pressure system over Iceland (the Icelandic Low) and a semi-permanent high pressure system over Bermuda (the Bermuda High). The interactions between these two systems have the power to alter storm tracks across the North Atlantic. When the pressure difference between these two systems is high, the NAO is in positive mode, resulting in relatively milder temperatures and decreased storm activity in Maine. When the pressure difference between the Icelandic Low and the Bermuda High is low, the NAO is in negative mode, which often brings cold temperatures and increased storm activity to Maine. NAO modes are long-term trends that can last for decades, and the present NAO mode has been mostly positive since the late 1970s.

Reading the Wind

Although weather conditions in Maine can change at a moment's notice, you can still get a general sense of what lies ahead by doing what sailors have done for hundreds of years: reading the wind.

During the summer, western winds generally bring sunny days. Winds that blow from the southwest bring warm, dry air, while winds that blow from the northwest bring cool, dry air, sweeping away moisture and creating spectacular visibility.

Winds that blow from the east are far less desirable. Southeasterly winds often bring overcast days with the possibility of drizzle and fog. And if the wind starts blowing from the northeast, batten down the hatches! A dreaded nor'easter could be on the way.

Although most common in the winter, nor'easters can happen at any time of the year. They form when cold, arctic air blowing down from Canada collides with warm, tropical air moving up the East Coast. The collision creates a counterclockwise spinning cyclone that's similar to a hurricane. As the cyclone moves offshore, winds arrive from the northeast—hence the term "nor'easter." When nor'easters form offshore, they can bring gale force winds, extreme surf, and massive amounts of rain, sleet, or snow. Remember *The Perfect Storm*? That was an offshore nor'easter. Onshore nor'easters are much less catastrophic, with many behaving like regular storms.

"Nor'easter" or "No-theaster"?

Today nearly everyone calls them nor'easters. But punctilious old salts claim the original word, as spoken by true Mainers, was "no-theaster." Back then, the distinction was critical in life-or-death situations, because "nor'east" might be mistaken for "nor'west," especially when wind, waves, and Maine accents were taken into account.

MAINE WINDS

SW

Warm, Dry Air

NW

Cool, Dry Air

SE

Cloudy, Rainy

NE

Nor'easter

COASTAL FOG

Fog is a fact of life in Downeast Maine, which typically sees 55 or more foggy days each year. (Locals sometimes refer to August as "Fogust.") Fog is essentially a cloud that forms at ground level when moist air cools to the dew point. Along the coast there are two common types of fog: evaporation fog and advection fog. Evaporation fog, also known as "sea smoke," forms in the winter when frigid air flows over the ocean. As ocean water evaporates into the frigid air, the air saturates and condenses. Sea smoke is light and thin and generally burns off by late morning. Advection fog, on the other hand, forms when warm and cold air interact. This happens in the summer when cool, moist air from the ocean blows over the heated land. It also happens offshore when warm, moist air from the Gulf Stream comes into contact with cold air in the Gulf of Maine. This is the classic pea-soup fog, and it can blow in from the ocean and linger along the coast for days. As one Maine sea captain put it in the 1800s, "You'll find fogs all the world over, but the Gulf Stream fog beats 'em all. It will heave in sooner, stay longer, and become thicker, and go away quicker than any fog I ever met in my voyaging."

One Perfect Day
on Mount Desert Island

- Sunrise on Cadillac Mountain (p.178)
- Breakfast at Cafe This Way or Two Cats (p.235)
- Midmorning walk on the Bar Harbor Shore Path (p.225)
- Late-morning drive along the Park Loop Road (p.137)
- Lunch at the Jordan Pond House (p.166)
- Rent bikes (p.232) and explore the carriage roads (p.199)
- Sunset at Bass Harbor Lighthouse (p.266)
- Dinner at Thurston's Lobster Pound (p.265)

One Perfect Day
for the Outdoor Buff

- Granola bar breakfast
- Sunrise at Egg Rock Overlook (p.147)
- Early Morning hike up the Precipice (p.184)
- Late Morning Hike up the Beehive (p.182)
- Lunch at Michelle's Brown Bag (p.236)
- Afternoon Sea Kayaking (p.23).
- Sunset on Cadillac Mountain (p.178)
- Dinner at Rosalie's Pizza ($) (p.236) or Mache ($$$) (p.235)
- Cold Bar Harbor Real Ale at the Lompoc Cafe (p.237)

Rainy Day Options

Here in Maine, rainy days are a fact of life. There is no "wet" or "dry" season in New England, unlike many other parts of the country. But although rainy days can happen anytime, there are plenty of indoor activities on Mount Desert Island.

MUSEUMS

Abbe Museum (p.228)

Bar Harbor Historical Society (p.229)

Bar Harbor Oceanarium (p.228)

Bar Harbor Whale Museum (p.228)

Dorr Museum at the College of the Atlantic (p.229)

Great Harbor Maritime Museum (p.246)

Mount Desert Island Historical Society (p.253)

Old School House & Museum (p.246)

Petit Plaisance (p.246)

Seal Cove Auto Museum (p.253)

Wendell Gilley Museum (p.257)

MOVIES & ENTERTAINMENT

Criterion Theater (p.233)

Reel Pizza Movie Theater (p.233)

ImprovAcadia (p.233)

Atlantic Brewing Company Tour (p.50)

What is Downeast Maine?

Downeast Maine refers to the state's northeast coastal region between Penobscot Bay and Canada. The term "Downeast" is derived from sailing terminology. Because the region's prevailing winds blow from the west, and because the coast of Maine trends northeast, ships sailing from Boston to Maine would sail *downwind* to travel *east*. Hence, Downeast. Likewise, ships sailing from Maine to Boston would sail upwind, which explains why many Mainers still say they're going "up to Boston" even though Boston is south of Maine.

Seasonal Festivals & Events

After emerging from its winter slumber, Mount Desert Island is awash with festivals in the spring, summer, and fall. Check local newspapers and publications for exact festival dates.

LEGACY OF THE ARTS FESTIVAL (June)

This week-long festival, held every year in late June, features exhibits, workshops, and an art show on the Village Green. (www.legacyartsfestival.com)

FOURTH OF JULY

This is the biggest celebration of the year in Bar Harbor, and it's always bursting with small town charm. Events include a pancake breakfast, morning parade, afternoon lobster bake, "lobster races" where live lobsters race each other in specially designed saltwater tanks, and evening fireworks at the town pier.

BAR HARBOR TOWN BAND (July, August)

The Bar Harbor Town Band offers free concerts at 8pm on Mondays and Thursdays in July and August at the bandstand on Village Green.

HARBOR HOUSE FLAMINGO FESTIVAL (July)

Southwest Harbor's annual plastic pink flamingo-themed festival is quite a sight. Don Featherstone, the inventor of the pink plastic flamingo, presides over the parade. Food and music events are also scheduled.

BAR HARBOR MUSIC FESTIVAL (July)

Since 1967 the Bar Harbor Music Festival has been organizing weekend concerts featuring classical, jazz, and pop. Times and locations vary, so call or check the schedule online. (207-288-5744, www.barharbormusicfestival.org)

NATIVE AMERICAN FESTIVAL (July)

This annual festival, co-sponsored by the Abbe Museum, is held the first Saturday after the fourth of July at the College of the Atlantic. It features baskets, beadwork, drumming, and dancing.

OPEN GARDEN DAY (July)

Every other year, members of the Mount Desert Garden Club showcase their private gardens in late July. (www.gcmdgardenday.com)

LOBSTER BOAT RACES (August)

Lobster boat races are a summer tradition along the coast of Maine, and the closest race to Mount Desert Island is in Winter Harbor near Schoodic Peninsula on the mainland. (www.lobsterboatracing.com)

ACADIA NIGHT SKY FESTIVAL (September)

The dark skies of Downeast Maine, delightfully free of urban light pollution, make it one of the best places on the East Coast for stargazing. The Acadia Night Sky Festival celebrates this fact with a variety of programs. (www.nightskyfestival.org)

GARLIC FESTIVAL (September)

In late September food lovers unite for a celebration of food, beer, wine, and garlic at Smuggler's Den Campground (www.nostrano.com)

OKTOBERFEST (October)

Every October nearly two dozen Maine breweries descend on Southwest Harbor for the town's annual Oktoberfest celebration at Smuggler's Den Campground.

MDI MARATHON (October)

The island's annual marathon always draws a crowd. (www.mdimarathon.org)

Local Publications

Mount Desert Island has two weekly newspapers: the **Bar Harbor Times** and **The Islander**. Both focus on local news, but in the summer there are plenty of articles geared towards visitors. Both papers feature a useful weekly calendar of events that list upcoming festivals, concerts, lectures, and more. The Bar Harbor Times puts its "Coming Events" in the center of the paper, and the Islander has its "Calendar" inside the Arts section.

Acadia National Park publishes the bi-monthly **Beaver Log**, which includes info such as tide charts, sunrise/sunset times, and a calendar of free ranger programs. A separate guide for the Island Explorer shuttle lists routes and schedules.

There are also several free advertiser-supported publications on the island. As long as you take their commercial recommendations with a grain of salt, these publications often offer some good local info.

Finally, if you're interested in general coastal Maine news, look for a copy of **The Working Waterfront**. This excellent free monthly paper, published by the Island Institute (p.46), focuses on fishing, fishermen, and Maine island life.

Bugs

Mosquitoes and tiny biting midges (aka "no-see-ums") are the most common bugs encountered on Mount Desert Island. The number of biting bugs varies each year depending on how much rain falls (more rain, more bugs), but bugs are most common in spring and early summer. If you plan on hiking, biking, or walking through the woods, it's always a good idea to bring bug spray with DEET. If you do find yourself covered with red, itchy bug bites, buy hydrocortisone cream (1%) and apply it to the bites.

Charitable Organizations

Acadia, the first national park created entirely from privately donated land, would not exist without the generosity of others. It was the foresight, activism, and financial contributions of the island's wealthy residents that preserved one of America's most spectacular landscapes nearly 100 years ago, and today that spirit of charitable giving continues. The following organizations all offer fantastic ways to give back to Acadia and help protect the coast of Maine for future generations.

FRIENDS OF ACADIA

This powerhouse non-profit, founded in 1986, works in tandem with the national park service to help preserve and protect Acadia National Park. FOA has raised millions of dollars to maintain Acadia's hiking trails and carriage roads in perpetuity, and it was a driving force behind the Island Explorer shuttle system. FOA also organizes volunteer programs and lobbying efforts on behalf of the park. (www.friendsofacadia.org)

ALLIED WHALE

This marine mammal research center, affiliated with Bar Harbor's College of the Atlantic, conducts conservation research on marine mammal populations and their habitats. Founded in 1972, it has been at the forefront of whale research for decades. To learn more visit the Bar Harbor Whale Museum (p.228) (www.coa.edu/html/allied-whale-microsite.htm)

MAINE COAST HERITAGE TRUST

Founded in 1970, the MCHT was a pioneer in using conservation easements to put permanent development restrictions on private land (often in exchange for tax breaks). To date it has protected over 130,000 acres in Maine, including more than 275 entire islands and 3,000 acres on Mount Desert Island. (www.mcht.org)

ISLAND INSTITUTE

This community development organization, founded in 1983, focuses on preserving the ecological and cultural heritage of Maine's 15 remaining year-round island communities. Five of those islands—Islesford, Great Cranberry Island, Frenchboro, Swan's Island, and Isle au Haut—lie within sight of Mount Desert Island. (www.islandinstitute.org)

NATURE CONSERVANCY

This global non-profit, founded in 1956 by a group that included Rachel Carson, helps protect natural places around the world, including over one million acres in Maine. Several islands near Mount Desert Island are protected by the Nature Conservancy, including Great Duck Island and Placentia Island. (www.nature.org)

Blueberry Bushes, Fall

LOCAL FOOD

MAINE LOBSTER

The Gulf of Maine is home to the freshest, tastiest lobster on the planet, so don't even think about visiting Mount Desert Island without sampling the state's quintessential crustacean. In addition to being tasty, lobster meat is virtually fat free. It has fewer calories and less cholesterol than chicken or beef, and it's full of vitamins A, B12, E, and Omega-3 fatty acids. (For more on lobsters see page 72).

While there are plenty of restaurants that serve up expensive, multi-course lobster dinners on Mount Desert Island, you'll find the freshest, best lobster at rough-around-the-edges lobster shacks where you can personally pick your critter from salt water tanks built into the counter. Don't be fooled by appearances. These raggedy seafood shrines are as good as it gets.

Best Authentic Lobster Meal: Thurston's Lobster Pound (p.265). Like any true lobster shack, Thurston's is a ramshackle affair. But the fresh lobster and gorgeous waterfront views of Bass Harbor can't be beat.

Second Best Authentic Lobster Meal: Captain's Galley at Beal's (p.259). Beal's is another diamond in the rough where the emphasis is on the fresh, quality lobster.

Best Lobster Dish: Lobster Crepes at Maggie's (p.235).

Worst Lobster Dish: Ben & Bill's Lobster Ice Cream (Bar Harbor). Ben & Bill's tried to take this appalling ice cream off their menu a few years back, but the public outcry was so great they put it back on the menu. If you really want to try it, ask for a free sample.

WILD BLUEBERRIES

After lobsters, wild blueberries are Maine's most famous natural delicacy. Maine leads the nation in wild blueberry production, and over 40,000 acres of wild blueberries are harvested within 60 miles of Mount Desert Island.

Although smaller than cultivated blueberries, wild blueberries are sweeter and tastier. They also contain nearly twice the antioxidants of cultivated berries. Studies have also indicated that a diet rich in wild blueberries may help improve memory.

Maine's official state berry is one of a handful of berry species native to North America (cranberries, strawberries, and raspberries are others). Blueberries were an important food for Indians, who combined dried blueberry powder with cornmeal, honey, and water to make a pudding called "Sautauthig." They also brewed a strong, aromatic tea from the root of the blueberry bush.

In 1822 Abijah Tabbutt, of Sugar Hill, Maine, invented the Blueberry Rake, a hand-held harvesting tool that looks like a metal dustpan with rounded teeth. Tabbutt's invention led to wide scale cultivation of Maine's vast blueberry fields, but it wasn't until the Civil War that the berry became famous outside New England. During the Civil War, scurvy-ravaged Union troops were in desperate need of vitamin C. Maine sardine canneries were converted to blueberry canneries and the vitamin-rich blueberries were sent south. As the berries spread across the country, so did their fame.

Today Maine harvests over 60 million pounds of wild blueberries each year. Each spring over 30 million bee hives, each containing 30,000 to 100,000 bees, are brought to Maine to pollinate the blueberry fields. Harvest season starts in late July/early August and runs through the first heavy frost in September or October. These days blueberry picking machines harvest most of the crop, while migrant workers rake the areas that machines can't reach. After the berries have been picked, the bushes' green leaves turn fiery red in the fall.

Wild blueberry bushes grow like weeds throughout Mount Desert Island, turning Acadia's mountains into massive, all-you-can eat buffets in late summer. During this time wild blueberries also spring up in supermarkets and roadside stands. In my experience, Ellsworth is the best place to buy wild blueberries from roadside stands. (Roadside stands near Mount Desert Island tend to be more expensive). Buy a bunch and freeze them for later. (And here's an old Maine trick: spread the berries out on a cookie tray, freeze them, and then put them in a plastic bag. That way the blueberries won't clump together when you take them out of the bag.)

LOCAL BREWS

It has been said that Bar Harbor has more microbreweries per capita than any other town in the United States. And while that only translates to three breweries (the town has a rather small capita), all three are great. There's nothing like finishing a hard day of hiking or sea kayaking with a frosty, local microbrew. My personal favorite: Atlantic Brewing Company's Bar Harbor Real Ale, which outsells all other beers on Mount Desert Island. And if you happen to visit Mount Desert Island in mid-October, be sure to check out Southwest Harbor's annual Oktoberfest, a day-long celebration that features beers from over two dozen Maine microbreweries.

Atlantic Brewing Company

This is the largest, most famous brewer on the island. Tours of their brewery, located a few miles east of downtown Bar Harbor between Route 3 and Route 102, are offered three times daily at 2pm, 3pm, and 4pm.
(207-288-2337, www.atlanticbrewing.com)

Bar Harbor Brewing Company

What started as a small husband-and-wife brewing operation has won numerous awards at the World Beer Championships. Visit their showroom at 8 Mount Desert Street, Bar Harbor, and try a free sample of their famous Thunder Hole Ale or Cadillac Mountain Stout.
(207-288-4592,www.barharborbrewing.com)

Maine Coast Brewing Company

This traditional English-style brewery offers a wide selection of handcrafted beers and seasonal brews. You can sample their beers at Jack Russell's Steakhouse, 102 Eden Street, Route 3, Bar Harbor.
(207-288-4914, www.bhmaine.com/MCBCPrimary.html)

Best Watering Holes on Mount Desert Island

If you immediately flipped to the previous page, you're my kind of reader. Which is to say, the kind of person who might appreciate the following list.

Best Classy Waterfront Cocktails

Terrace Grille at the Bar Harbor Inn, Bar Harbor (p.237)
Perched on the lawn in front of the elegant Bar Harbor Inn, this outdoor restaurant offers terrific views of Frenchman Bay.

The Boathouse at the Claremont Inn, Southwest Harbor (p.257)
The historic Claremont Inn, the oldest hotel on the island, serves delicious, creative cocktails from the "boathouse" next to their private pier.

Best Laid Back Waterfront Cocktails

Fish House Grill, Bar Harbor (p.237)
Located next to the Bar Harbor Pier, the Fish House has outdoor picnic tables where you can kick back and observe the hustle of the harbor.

Moorings Restaurant, Southwest Harbor (131 Shore Road, 207-244-7070)
Situated directly across from the dramatic entrance to Somes Sound, this restaurant might have my favorite waterfront view on the island.

Sea Food Ketch, Bass Harbor (p.265)
Famous for their outdoor patio with terrific views of Bass Harbor.

Islesford Dock Restaurant, Islesford (p.272)
For a totally unique cocktail experience, catch a ferry to Islesford and take in the view of Acadia's mountains from an offshore island.

Other Notable Bars

Best for Dancing: Carmen Verandah, Bar Harbor (p.233)
Best for Local Color: Thirsty Whale, Bar Harbor (p.233)
Best for Hippies & Outdoorsy Folk: Lompoc Cafe, Bar Harbor (p.233)
Best Sports Bar: Little Anthony's, Bar Harbor (p.233)

GEOLOGY

Mount desert island is one of the most fascinating geologic features on the eastern seaboard. Unlike much of the East Coast, which is sandy and flat, Mount Desert Island towers 1,500 feet above a rocky shore. No fewer than 26 mountain peaks rise above the island, some visible up to 60 miles at sea. How these mountains formed is a fascinating story that involves colliding continents, erupting volcanoes, scouring glaciers, and countless other splendid catastrophes. The result: one of the most beautiful islands in the North Atlantic.

Five hundred million years ago, Maine was covered by an ancient ocean that pre-dated the modern Atlantic. Geologists call this ocean the Iapetus Ocean (Iapetus was the father of Atlas, "Atlantic"). As ancient rivers flowed into the Iapetus Ocean, vast amounts of sediment accumulated offshore. This sediment—a combination of sand, mud, and silt—piled up in thick layers, and over millions of years the bottom layers were compressed into sedimentary rock. As tectonic plates shifted, this newly formed rock was pushed deep below the surface of the Earth where extreme heat and pressure transformed it into schist, a metamorphic rock similar to slate. The schist that formed is called Ellsworth schist, and it is the oldest rock found on Mount Desert Island.

After the Ellsworth schist formed, tectonic action pushed it near the surface where it became the floor of the Iapetus Ocean. As rivers from ancient continents deposited fresh sediments into the Iapetus Ocean around 420 million years ago, a new layer of sedimentary rocks formed on top of the Ellsworth schist. These new sedimentary rocks are called the Bar Harbor Formation. Roughly 20 million years later, a string of volcanic islands formed in the Iapetus Ocean. Ash from the erupting volcanoes settled on top of the Bar Harbor Formation, forming a third set of rocks: the Cranberry Isles Series.

Around 400 million years ago, the three oldest rocks on Mount Desert Island— Ellsworth schist, Bar Harbor Formation, and Cranberry Isles Series—had formed. At this point all three rocks were part of an ancient continent called Avalonia, lying somewhere between North America and Europe in the Iapetus Ocean. But slowly, as tectonic plates shifted, North America and Avalonia started moving toward each other, and eventually the two continents collided.

The collision pushed up a massive mountain chain and caused huge pools of magma to rise up under the previously formed Avalonian rocks. Around 360 million years ago the magma cooled into granite, creating the fourth (and most famous) rock formation on Mount Desert Island. But at this point all four rocks were still buried deep underground.

AVALONIA

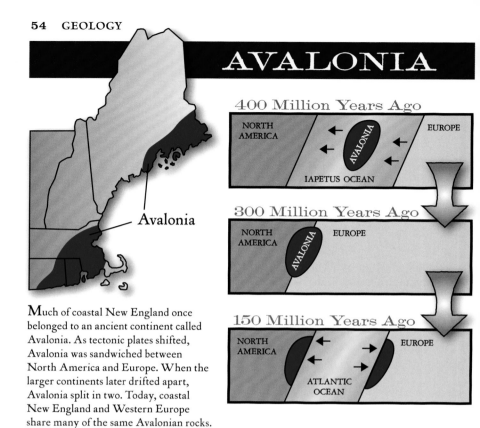

400 Million Years Ago

NORTH AMERICA · AVALONIA · EUROPE · IAPETUS OCEAN

300 Million Years Ago

NORTH AMERICA · AVALONIA · EUROPE

150 Million Years Ago

NORTH AMERICA · EUROPE · ATLANTIC OCEAN

Avalonia

Much of coastal New England once belonged to an ancient continent called Avalonia. As tectonic plates shifted, Avalonia was sandwiched between North America and Europe. When the larger continents later drifted apart, Avalonia split in two. Today, coastal New England and Western Europe share many of the same Avalonian rocks.

Although geologists know a good deal about rock formation on Mount Desert Island between 500 and 350 million years ago, the last 350 million years are a bit of a mystery. Any evidence indicating what kind of landscape existed here has long since eroded away. They do know, however, that after the collision of North America and Avalonia, Africa and Eurasia smashed into North America to form a huge supercontinent called Pangea. These collisions also pushed up the Appalachian Mountains. At this point Maine was located near the geographic center of Pangea—a position close to the equator that created a warm, tropical climate.

Then, around 200 million years ago, Pangea started to break apart. Around 150 million years ago Avalonia split in two with the western portion stuck to North America and the eastern portion stuck to Europe. (Even today, coastal Maine and Western Europe share many of the same Avalonian rocks.) As North America and Europe drifted apart, the Atlantic Ocean was born and North America moved north from the equator to its present location. During this time erosion slowly chipped away the landscape to reveal the rocks that would ultimately form Mount Desert Island. But it would take one last dramatic act of geology before the island took on the familiar profile we know today.

THE ICE AGE

AROUND TWO MILLION years ago, Earth entered the Ice Age and thick layers of snow accumulated in the arctic that compacted into massive sheets of ice. Soon the ice sheets were set into motion under the pressure of their own weight, at which point they became glaciers. Pushing south, the glaciers consumed everything in their path. Boulders, soil, trees—everything but the bedrock was picked up and carried along.

But even the bedrock did not escape unscathed. The glaciers, essentially dirty ice full of loose debris, acted like giant sheets of sandpaper, grinding down the bedrock and smoothing it out. The glaciers advanced over much of North America, then retreated abruptly. Then they advanced and retreated again. Then they advanced and retreated nearly a dozen more times. The most recent glacial cycle ended around 12,000 years ago.

Scientists are unsure what triggered the Ice Age (a period we are still in today) or why glacial advance has followed a somewhat predictable cycle. One culprit seems to be a small wobble in the earth's orbit that affects how much solar radiation reaches the Earth. When the wobble goes one way, solar radiation increases, temperatures rise, snowfall decreases, and the glaciers melt. When the wobble goes the other way, solar radiation decreases, temperatures drop, snowfall increases, and the glaciers advance. This cycle—earth wobbling, glaciers advancing, Earth wobbling, glaciers retreating—generally lasts about 120,000 years. Cool periods of glacial advance last about 100,000 years with warmer, interglacial periods of about 10,000 to 20,000 years in between. (We are currently about 15,000 years into the current interglacial period.)

Prior to the Ice Age, Mount Desert Island had been home to a series of jagged granite mountains separated by steep, V-shaped valleys cut by streams over millions of years. When the glaciers arrived, they flowed into the V-shaped valleys and gouged them out into graceful U-shaped valleys. Soon only jagged mountain peaks stuck out of the glacier like rocky islands in a sea of ice. As the glacier continued to advance, even the peaks disappeared under the ice, and the jagged mountain peaks were rounded down to the graceful shapes we know today.

The most recent period of glacial advance started about 100,000 years ago. Around 25,000 years ago, massive glaciers had reached the coast of Maine. And at the glacier's maximum extent, roughly 18,000 years ago, Mount Desert Island was buried under several thousand feet of ice. The glacier covered every mountain in New England, stretched 350 miles past the present shoreline, and reached as far south as Long Island. So much of the world's water was frozen in glaciers that global ocean levels dropped roughly 300 feet. And the tremendous weight of the glacier (one cubic mile of ice weighs 4.5 billion tons) compressed the land at least 600 feet below present-day levels.

Then, around 18,000 years ago, Earth's temperatures warmed and the glacier started to melt. Within 5,000 years the glacier had retreated as far as central Maine. Three thousand years later it had disappeared entirely from the state. The melting glacier released massive amounts of water, forming huge rivers that raced to the sea and cut deep channels into the land. Many of those Ice Age channels continue to guide the paths of major rivers flowing through present-day Maine.

As water returned to the sea, ocean levels rose roughly 300 feet, flooding the compressed land and sending saltwater up to 60 miles inland in Maine. But free of the weight of the glaciers, the compressed land slowly rebounded and rose back toward its original levels, draining the interior of the state and forming the modern shoreline. Remnants of the former high shoreline can still be found on the mountains of Mount Desert Island, including cobblestone beaches stranded high above the present sea level.

Before the Ice Age, the coast of Maine was covered in sandy beaches—the result of waves grinding down a once rocky shore. But when glaciers descended, they pushed the sand and other sediments out to sea and permanently tilted the land near the coast, which was covered in rolling hills before the Ice Age. When ocean levels rose, those tilted hills, scraped bare by the glacier, formed the hundreds of rocky inlets and bays that now make up the present shoreline.

Today, elements such as rain, ice, and waves continue to chip away at Mount Desert Island. Some geologists estimate that erosion removes about two inches from the island every 1,000 years. A million years from now, the forces of geology will have rendered Mount Desert Island completely unrecognizable to modern eyes. In the meantime, it remains one of the most beautiful places in the world.

GEORGES BANK

Roughly 18,000 years ago, when a vast glacier extended nearly 350 miles past the present Maine shoreline, the front of the glacier pushed a vast accumulation of rocks and loose debris. When the glacier retreated, the debris was left behind to form what geologists call a terminal moraine. At the start of the glacier's retreat, sea levels were roughly 200 feet below present levels, and the terminal moraine formed a gravelly ridge connected to the mainland. But as the massive glacier melted, ocean levels rose and flooded the terminal moraine, creating a shallow underwater ridge that today is known as Georges Bank. (Another part of the terminal moraine, Cape Cod, still remains above sea level.) Georges Bank is one of the defining features of the Gulf of Maine, effectively separating the Gulf from the open Atlantic. And from time to time fishing trawls on Georges Bank have dragged up mammoth bones and other remnants of Ice Age creatures that roamed there thousands of years ago.

ICE AGE GLACIERS

North America
18,000 years ago

At the peak of the last Ice Age, North America was covered by an enormous glacier that held 1.5 times more ice than is found on Antarctica today. At the time, Mount Desert Island was buried under several thousand feet of ice, which was so heavy that it compressed the land. At the glacier's maximum extent, it stretched roughly 350 miles into the Gulf of Maine.

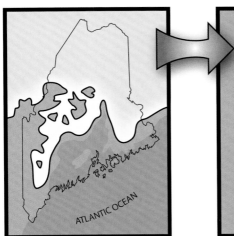

ATLANTIC OCEAN

ATLANTIC OCEAN

13,000 years ago

As temperatures on Earth continue to rise, the glacier continues to melt and retreat. The huge volumes of melting ice cause sea levels to rise, flooding the compressed land in Maine.

11,000 years ago

Free of the weight of the glaciers, the land in Maine rises and drains. But with so much ocean water still trapped in retreating glaciers, sea levels remain below present-day levels.

ECOLOGY

From an ecological standpoint, Acadia is one of the most diverse national parks in America. With elevations ranging from sea-level to 1,500 feet, a location at the boundary of two of North America's major botanical zones, and a landscape filled with forests, lakes, and wetlands, Acadia is home to an astonishing number of plants and animals. All told, over 50 species of mammals, 320 species of birds, and 1,000 species of flowering plants have been identified in the park (as well as hundreds of creatures in the waters offshore). Even more amazing, Acadia's species are all found on less than 48,000 acres. Outside of a tropical rainforest, there are few places in the world with so much natural diversity packed into such a small space.

Mount Desert Island lies at the boundary of North America's northern boreal forest, found in northern Maine and much of Canada, and eastern deciduous forest, found in southern Maine and over much of the eastern U.S. The boreal forest is dominated by evergreens such as red spruce and balsam fir. Both are hardy trees that can establish themselves in thin, poor soil. Thriving in damp, cool climates, they create a dense canopy that blocks sunlight and drops needles that create an acidic soil. As a result, spruce-fir forests tend to go unchallenged by other trees that require abundant sunlight and rich soil to grow. The nutrient-poor floor of spruce-fir forests is often covered with mosses and lichens.

In 1947 a fire burned nearly half of the eastern side of Mount Desert Island, clearing out 17,000 acres of spruce-fir forest and allowing deciduous trees like birch, poplar, oak, and other hardwoods to grow. In contrast to the boreal forest, deciduous trees drop leaves that enrich the soil and allow other plants to grow. Today, over 30 different tree species are found on Mount Desert Island, including pitch pines growing at the northeastern limit of their range and jack pines growing at the southern limit of their range. Scattered among the trees are over 40 kinds of shrubs and hundreds of smaller plants like wildflowers, shrubs, and ferns.

Hike up the island's tallest mountains and the forests soon give way to rocky peaks. Here, small populations of alpine plants eke out a living in tiny pockets of soil. Because there is so little vegetation on the mountain peaks, there is very little soil development—a self-reinforcing process that prevents many larger plants like trees from taking root. Lying exposed at high elevations, the peaks experience cooler than average year-round temperatures. This creates an excellent habitat for several rare species of plants normally found much farther north, including Alpine clubmoss and mountain sandwort.

During the summer, the island's mountains are often bathed in thick fog, which provides moisture for the plants near the summit. Any rain that falls tends to rush off the peaks immediately because there is so little vegetation to absorb the water or slow it down. As the water cascades down the rocks, it often forms dozens of temporary waterfalls. The water then gathers into numerous streams that flow into the island's lakes, ponds and marshes.

Roughly 20 percent of Acadia is considered wetland, habitats that include salt-water marshes, freshwater marshes, bogs and swamps. Because wetlands attract plants and animals from both land and water, they are extremely important to the park's ecology. They are among the most biodiverse of all ecosystems, and wetlands provide important stopover points for birds migrating on the Atlantic flyway.

Mount Desert Island is considered one of America's premier birding locations. James Audubon, founder of the Audubon Society, did much of his research here, and birders from around the world continue to flock to Acadia. Lying on the boundary of North America's temperate and sub-arctic zone, the island attracts over 330 species of birds, many of which arrive in the spring. Among the spring arrivals are 21 species of nesting wood warblers, earning Acadia the nickname "Warbler Capital of North America." The fall migration also attracts a variety of interesting birds, but by winter Mount Desert Island's bird population has been reduced to a fraction of its summertime high. Still, winter brings some fascinating migrants from the far north and arctic, including snowy owls, great gray owls, and king eiders.

Due to its coastal location, Mount Desert Island is also within range of many fascinating seabirds. Some, such as Leach's storm petrel, spend much of their lives on the open ocean, and they are rarely seen from land. Others, like common eiders and guillemots, can be spotted bobbing in the surf just off Mount Desert Island.

Mount Desert Island is also home to a wide range of mammals. Some, such as snowshoe hares and white-tailed deer, are strict vegetarians, nibbling on grasses and shrubs. Others, such as red foxes and eastern coyotes, are predators that feed on smaller animals. Acadia also contains 11 of Maine's 19 amphibian species, including 6-inch bullfrogs and the thumbnail-sized spring peeper, a tree frog that chirps up to 4,500 times per night in the spring. But because Mount Desert Island is located so far north, there are very few reptiles, which are cold-blooded and prefer a warmer climate. Only two species of turtle and five species of snake, none of which are poisonous, are found in the park.

In addition to land on Mount Desert Island, Acadia National Park also includes many smaller offshore islands. Characterized by cool climates and rocky terrain, these islands feature a habitat similar to Acadia's mountain peaks, well suited to sub-arctic plants and animals normally found much farther north. The lack of predators on many offshore islands also provides excellent breeding sites for seabirds. Great Duck Island, 6 miles south of Mount Desert Island, supports 20 percent of Maine's nesting seabirds, and Petit Manan Island, 16 miles to the east, is home to a breeding colony of puffins.

FALL FOLIAGE

New England is famous for its fall foliage, and here in Acadia the changing leaves are particularly dramatic. But what causes the leaves to change? The answer is chlorophyll—or rather, lack of chlorophyll. In the spring, new leaves contain a variety of pigments—red, yellow, orange, purple—but chlorophyll's green pigment is always dominant in the spring and summer when the leaves photosynthesize. When the days grow shorter in the fall, chlorophyll production drops and the green pigment starts to fade. Ultimately the green pigment disappears entirely, and the leaves' other colorful pigments are gloriously revealed.

Amazingly, we have Florida to thank for New England's famous foliage. Twenty thousand years ago, advancing glaciers had pushed all of North America's ecosystems hundreds of miles south. As the glaciers advanced, New England's famous deciduous trees migrated all the way down the eastern seaboard, and ultimately they were pushed to the tip of Florida. Had Florida not existed, it's possible that the trees might have been pushed to extinction. But when temperatures warmed and the glaciers retreated, the trees slowly migrated back to New England.

Peak foliage on Mount Desert Island usually occurs in mid-October, but the exact timing varies from year to year depending on the amount of heat and rain in summer and early fall. For up-to-the-minute foliage conditions and forecasts, visit www.mainefoliage.com.

Barnacles & Dog Whelks

INTERTIDAL ZONE

WHEN PEOPLE THINK of marine ecology, they often picture fish, whales and other creatures of the open sea. But between the ocean and the land lies another amazing ecosystem: the intertidal zone. This fascinating region, encompassing the shore between high and low tide, is a world unto itself. Creatures living here have adapted to a brutal environment where they must cope with life above and below water, tolerate extreme temperature fluctuations, and survive the violent pounding of the waves. During winter storms, waves in the intertidal zone can produce pressures up to 500 pounds per square inch!

Some of the most dynamic organisms on the planet are found in the intertidal zone, but much of this amazing landscape remains off limits to the public because so much of the Maine coast is privately owned. In Acadia National Park, however, over 40 miles of rocky shoreline are open to explore, revealing the wonders of this fascinating ecosystem. And due to the Gulf of Maine's unusually large tides (8–12 feet in Acadia), the intertidal zone here is particularly dramatic.

The intertidal zone is a complex ecosystem containing a wide range of sub-ecosystems. Near the top of the intertidal zone, organisms live most of their lives above water. Only at high tide are they fully submerged, and even then just for a few hours. At the bottom of the intertidal zone, organisms are only exposed to the air at low tide, and they have evolved accordingly. In fact, many organisms living at the bottom of the intertidal zone will die if exposed to the air for too long. In between these two extremes lies a wide range of plants and animals adapted to specific amounts of time both above and below water.

Perhaps no animal sums up the intertidal zone's evolutionary variety as perfectly as the periwinkle, a marine snail that grazes on algae. There are three types of periwinkles in Acadia, and all are adapted to different amounts of water. The smooth periwinkle spends most of its time below water and can't stand air. The common periwinkle can stand air, but not very much. And the rough periwinkle prefers air, needing water only occasionally. Both smooth and common periwinkles lay their eggs in the water, but rough periwinkle babies are born live on the rocks. In fact, some scientists believe rough periwinkles are slowly evolving into land snails. In the future, they may disappear from the intertidal zone entirely!

Tidepools along the rocky shore are some of the best places to explore the wonders of the intertidal zone. These temporary pockets of water are filled with life-forms as small as plankton and as large as starfish and sea anemones. But even tidepools are highly varied. The location of a tidepool within the intertidal zone has a dramatic effect on the plants and animals that can live there. Tidepools at the top of the intertidal zone experience drastic fluctuations in temperature, water level, and salinity as sunlight heats the pool and water evaporates throughout the day. By contrast, tidepools at the bottom of the intertidal zone are exposed to much less sunlight, and their fluctuations are much less severe.

INTERTIDAL ZONE

SPLASH ZONE: Although splashed by waves and spray at high tide, this zone is never fully submerged. It is sometimes called the Black Zone due to a dark algae that grows on the rocks, which is fed upon by small marine snails called rough periwinkles.

BARNACLE ZONE: This easily identified zone is home to countless tiny white barnacles, which spend their entire lives glued to a single location. When the tide is high, barnacles extend feathery legs to feed on floating food particles. When the tide is low, barnacles retract their legs and close a "trap door" at the tip of their conical shell.

ROCKWEED ZONE: Large strands of rubbery rockweeds cover this mid-intertidal zone. As the tide rises, tiny air bladders in the rockweeds lift them toward the surface where they can better photosynthesize. At low tide, rockweeds draped over the rocks provide moist protection for mussels, crabs, and dog whelks.

IRISH MOSS ZONE: This loosely defined zone often overlaps with the zones above and below it. Its namesake plant, Irish Moss, has beautiful iridescent tips and grows in small, dense clumps. Sea anemones, whose tentacles shoot microscopic spears that paralyze their victims with poison, are sometimes found in the Irish moss zone.

KELP ZONE: Thick curtains of kelp define the lowermost zone, which is home to such famous creatures as sea stars, sea urchins, and sea cucumbers. Kelp anchor themselves to the bottom and send up long, belt-like ribbons that can grow up to 20 feet.

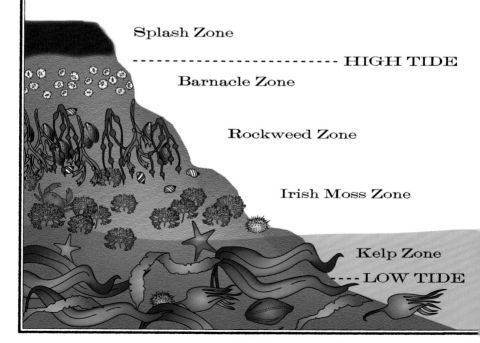

Splash Zone

-------------------------- HIGH TIDE

Barnacle Zone

Rockweed Zone

Irish Moss Zone

Kelp Zone

---- LOW TIDE

SEA STARS (*Asterias vulgaris*)

Sea stars (aka starfish) are found in the lower intertidal zones. They grow up to 10 inches across and come in a rainbow of colors. Their arms are covered with hundreds of tiny tube feet, which they use for movement and to pry open mussels. After opening a mussel, a sea star will disgorge its stomach into the open shell, digesting the victim from the inside. Sea stars can regenerate lost arms, and the tip of each arm has a tiny, primitive "eye."

DOG WHELK (*Thais lapillus*)

This predatory sea snail (distinguished by a pointed spire) roves around the mid-intertidal zone and feasts on stationary victims. Using a tongue-like organ called a radula, dog whelks drill into the shells of barnacles and mussels. It takes roughly one hour to drill into a barnacle and 10–20 hours to drill into a mussel. Digestive enzymes are then injected into the victim's shell, creating a soup that the dog whelk sucks out. Mussels sometimes fight back by attaching threads to the dog whelk, immobilizing it until it starves to death.

SEA CUCUMBER (*Cucumaria frondosa*)

These strange, leathery creatures, found in the lower intertidal zones, grow up to 10 inches long and filter out nutrients from ingested sediments. Sea cucumbers can loosen and firm their bodies at will. If a sea cucumber wants to squeeze through a small gap, it can essentially liquefy its body to do so. When seriously threatened, it disgorges its internal organs to confuse predators (new organs will later regenerate). Sea cucumbers "breath" by drawing water in and out of the anus.

SEA URCHIN (*Strongylocentrotus droebachiensis*)

These prickly creatures, found in the lower intertidal zones, have a spiny, limestone shell that protects their soft organs from predators. They use tiny tube feet to "walk" along the rocks as they graze on algae. Seagulls pluck urchins from the intertidal zone and drop them on rocks to crack open their hard shells.

GULF OF MAINE

PERHAPS THE MOST fascinating aspect of Acadia's ecology is the Gulf of Maine, a shallow region (on average 500 feet deep) that covers 69,000 square miles of the Atlantic Ocean from Cape Cod to Nova Scotia. About 200 miles from the coast lies the Gulf's most prominent physical feature: Georges Bank. Only 13 feet deep in places, Georges Bank is a 10,000 square-mile shallow ridge that acts as a barrier between the Gulf of Maine and the open Atlantic, creating a semi-enclosed sea with the help of Browns Bank to the northeast. Over 60 rivers flow into the Gulf of Maine, depositing an average of 250 billion gallons of freshwater each year. Georges Bank and Browns Bank help retain this freshwater to create, in effect, a massive estuary—a place where freshwater and saltwater mix that is extremely productive biologically.

In addition to the freshwater deposited by rivers, cold arctic ocean water is cycled into the Gulf of Maine via the Labrador Current, which flows south along the eastern coast of Nova Scotia. This cold, dense, nutrient-rich water enters the Gulf of Maine via the Northeastern Channel, a deep underwater valley between Georges Bank and Browns Bank. The Northeast Channel formed at the end of the last Ice Age, when so much of the world's water was frozen in glaciers that sea levels lay hundreds of feet below present levels. As global temperatures rose and the glaciers melted, a massive river flowed across the Gulf of Maine, which was then above sea level, and helped carve the deep valley that would ultimately become the Northeast Channel.

After nutrient-rich arctic water from the Labrador Current enters the Gulf of Maine, it settles in undersea basins up to 1,500 feet deep. During the winter, when the surface water cools to the upper 30s °F, the surface water sinks to the bottom and stirs up the arctic water. By the time spring arrives, the Gulf of Maine is swirling with nutrients. As the days grow longer, abundant sunlight triggers massive phytoplankton blooms, which give the Gulf of Maine its characteristic green, murky water. (A single teaspoon of Maine seawater can hold over a million phytoplankton.) The phytoplankton are then fed upon by tiny animals called zooplankton, which form the foundation of a thriving food chain.

Zooplankton are fed upon by small fish like herring and mackerel, which often school by the thousands. Those fish, in turn, are eaten by tuna, sharks, and migrating whales, who can eat up to 5,000 herring per day. Meanwhile, the unusually craggy floor of the Gulf of Maine makes ideal habitat for lobsters, and just above the seafloor are bottom dwelling fish such as cod, haddock, and flounder. All told, the Gulf of Maine is home to over 3,000 species, including 652 fish, 32 mammals, and over 700 species of microscopic plants.

In the summer, when surface temperatures warm to the mid-60s °F, convective mixing between the surface and the bottom slows. Nutrient-rich water settles to the bottom, and phytoplankton density drops. Closer to shore, however, dramatic

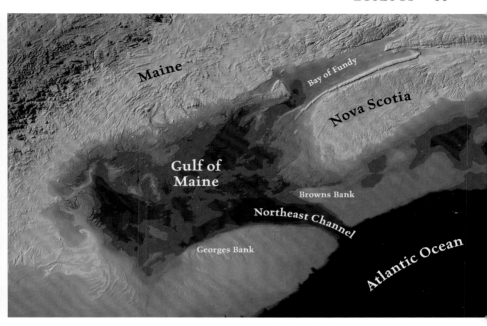

tides ensure continuous mixing of nutrients. Although tides rise and fall an average of three to six feet over much of the earth, in Maine tides can rise and fall up to 28 feet. Farther north in Canada's Bay of Fundy, a long channel connected to the northern tip of the Gulf of Maine, tides rise and fall an astonishing 50 feet—the largest tidal fluctuations in the world. The Bay of Fundy's stunning tides create, in effect, a giant nutrient pump. Twice a day, over 100 billion tons of water are sucked into the Bay of Fundy, then injected back into the Gulf of Maine.

The dramatic tides in the Gulf of Maine and the Bay of Fundy are due to the region's shallow underwater topography. As tides in the Atlantic rise and fall, water sloshes back and forth over the Gulf of Maine like water sloshing back and forth in a bathtub. Ultimately this sloshing water amplifies the tidal range, a phenomenon called tidal resonance. The unique shape of the Bay of Fundy has even greater tidal resonance, which accounts for its record setting tides.

The Gulf of Maine's high tides create abundant mixing close to shore, and sinking surface water in the winter stirs up deep nutrients offshore. But another natural feature mixes the water further still: a powerful counter-clockwise current that cycles around the entire Gulf of Maine every three months. The current not only ensures further mixing of nutrients, it disperses the eggs and larvae of numerous marine animals, scattering biodiversity throughout the Gulf.

Taken together, the unique aspects of the Gulf of Maine—its shallow depth, estuary-like quality, nutrient-rich waters, and multiple circulation patterns—have created one of the most productive ecosystems in the world. According to some scientists, the Gulf of Maine is richer in nutrients than almost any other place in the earth's oceans.

HUMAN IMPACT

A S EUROPEAN SETTLEMENT spread throughout coastal Maine in the late 1700s, settlers altered the environment in many significant ways. Although Indians had been altering the environment for centuries through hunting, harvesting, and intentional fires to clear brush, their activities—limited by small populations and a lack of technology—had a relatively minor impact on the land. But when European settlers arrived, their impact was swift and dramatic.

The most obvious change was to the forest. Oaks, cedars, and chestnuts were all harvested for shipbuilding and other construction, but the most important tree was the white pine, which grows up to 250 feet high and towers above all other trees in New England. Referred to as "skyscrapers" before steel buildings stole the name, white pines were perfect for ship masts. Before long, aggressive harvesting had wiped out the white pine population along the coast. As loggers pushed farther inland, settlers along the coast cleared out large swaths of the remaining forest to farm and graze cattle. By the mid-1800s much of the coast had been completely stripped of trees.

Human activities also took a huge toll on animal populations in coastal Maine. As trade between Indians and Europeans increased in the 1600s, Indians hunted animals in much larger numbers than their pre-contact lifestyles required. Soon, many animals, particularly beaver, had been hunted out of much of the region. Later, coastal residents began to hunt seabirds for their meat, eggs and feathers. Because seabirds reproduce in relatively small numbers, seabird hunting had devastating effects. One species, the penguin-like great auk, was hunted to extinction. Unable to fly away from humans, great auks were simply rounded up on shore and clubbed to death. Ultimately public pressure, including the founding of the National Audubon Society, encouraged protection of the remaining seabird population. The landmark Migratory Bird Treaty Act of 1918 banned seabird hunting, and many bird sanctuaries were established along the coast of Maine. Over time, many seabird populations have slowly recovered.

On Mount Desert Island, the environment has also been altered in more subtle ways. Today nearly one-quarter of the plants found in Acadia are non-native "exotics." Free from the diseases and pests that keep their populations in check back home, some exotics have thrived in Acadia. Purple loosestrife, a beautiful European plant with magenta flowers that bloom in July and August, has flourished in wetlands throughout the park and muscled out native plants. Within the boundaries of Acadia, purple loosestrife populations are kept under strict control, but outside the park the plant is thriving. About a dozen other non-native species are currently considered a disturbance to the park's native ecosystem.

But the ecosystem most in peril these days is the Gulf of Maine. For centuries the Gulf of Maine was considered one of the richest offshore fisheries in the world.

But once-abundant fish such as cod, haddock, swordfish and bluefin tuna have seen their populations collapse over the past half century due to overfishing.

In the 1950s fears of a global food shortage were widespread, and the U.N. encouraged massive increases in fishing to avert the coming catastrophe. At the same time, modern fishing technology allowed catches to skyrocket—and skyrocket they did, particularly in the Gulf of Maine. In the 1960s dozens of industrial fishing vessels from the Soviet Union, Western Europe, and Japan arrived in the Gulf of Maine. At the time, the United States only had jurisdiction over waters within 12 miles of its coast. The foreign vessels, some up to 400 feet long, stayed for months at a time and hauled up astounding catches. In 1968 foreign vessels harvested 1.2 billion tons, compared to 556 million tons harvested by U.S. vessels.

Alarmed by the foreign harvests, Congress passed the Fisheries Conservation and Management Act in 1976, which extended control of U.S. waters from 12 to 200 miles offshore and prohibited foreign vessels from plundering the Gulf of Maine. The act did not, however, prohibit American vessels from plundering the Gulf of Maine, which is exactly what happened next. Government subsidies were created to expand the U.S. fishing fleet, and the massive harvests continued. Then, as powerful electronic fish finding technology was adopted in the 1980s, harvesting ability vastly exceeded available stocks, and by the end of the decade fish populations in the Gulf of Maine had collapsed.

In the 1990s environmental groups lobbied for, and achieved, strict fishing regulations to save the remaining fish. But the one-size-fits-all regulations were ill-suited to the complex, dynamic ecology of the Gulf of Maine and its wide variety of fishing vessels. The new regulations had the unintended consequence of actually incentivizing some unsustainable fishing practices, and they ultimately favored large fishing operations over small independent fishermen. Across Maine, small independent fisherman abandoned the fish species that had sustained their communities for generations and switched to lobster. This is the last commercial species in the Gulf of Maine whose population has remained healthy due to harvesting regulations put in place decades ago and the strong, conservation-minded ethos of the lobstermen. But dependence on a single species is fraught with hazard. Any disturbance to Maine's lobster harvests could jeopardize the state's entire fishing industry and wreak havoc on small coastal communities.

Meanwhile, the federal regulations put in place have failed to adequately rebuild fishing stocks. But after decades of mutual mistrust, some fisherman, lawmakers, and environmentalists could be at a turning point. They are starting to share the blame for past mistakes and work together to devise a new framework. Today many prominent thinkers have concluded that the top-down nature of federal regulations are clearly ineffective, and a new solution based on community-centered management practices and local stewardship is far more preferable. This radical idea, it turns out, is not so radical after all. It appears to have worked exceptionally well over the past several decades for Maine's signature marine species: lobster.

LOBSTERS

LOBSTERS ARE THE quintessential symbol of Maine. Although billboards are banned throughout the state, it's impossible to drive through a coastal town without being bombarded by dozens of images of lobsters. And rightly so. Although there are roughly 30 species of clawed lobsters in the world, no seafloor on the planet is as densely populated with lobsters as the Gulf of Maine. And the specific species found here, *Homarus americanus*, is one of the world's most unusual and fascinating creatures.

The American lobster is found on the ocean floor from North Carolina to Newfoundland, but they thrive in the Gulf of Maine due to its cold, shallow waters and rocky, craggy seafloor. Lobsters seek out shelter among the rocks, with large lobsters snagging the best hiding spots and vigorously defending them. Smaller lobsters are often forced to burrow into the sand like rodents. In some parts of the Gulf of Maine, the density of lobsters is roughly one per square meter.

Because lobsters are almost neutrally buoyant, they tiptoe across the bottom with ease. In the spring, millions of lobsters migrate towards the warmer waters closer to shore. In the fall, when water temperatures near the shore drop due to cold winds, lobsters crawl back to their warmer, deep water wintering grounds. Lobsters can travel up to four miles per day, and if threatened they can propel themselves backward more than 25 feet per second by flapping their powerful tail.

Young lobsters start out with two claws of equal size, but as they mature they develop a preference for one or the other, much as people become right- or left-handed. The preferred claw becomes the powerful "crusher" claw, which is used to crush the shells of victims. The smaller, "shredder" claw is used to tear and shred flesh. As food is brought close to the face, a vast array of tiny appendages near the mouth are employed as forks, clamps, brushes, and shredders. After the food is ingested, it is chewed in the stomach by three teeth-like grinders. Lobsters feed on just about anything, including mussels, crabs, and starfish. Lobsters, in turn, are preyed upon by skates, sharks, and groundfish that swallow them whole.

Because lobsters grow throughout their lives, they must periodically shed their shells to accommodate larger bodies. This process, called molting, is similar to how a snake sheds its skin. In a lobster's first five years, it will molt roughly 25 times, gaining 15 percent body length and 50 percent volume each time. As adults get larger, they molt fewer and fewer times. A three- to four-pound lobster may only molt every three to five years.

Prior to a molt, a new shell forms just under the lobster's old shell. The lobster then drains the remaining calcium out of its old shell and stores it in a reservoir to be recycled into the new shell. When the lobster is finally ready to molt, it secretes enzymes that soften the old shell, swells its body with saltwater, and splits the old shell open. The lobster then backs out of the old shell and attempts to pull its large claw muscles through the shell's narrow claw joints. Occasionally a claw muscle

won't fit through the old shell, and it is torn off in the process. But the claws, like all other lobster appendages, have the ability to regenerate over time. The entire molting process can take anywhere from five minutes to half an hour.

After a molt the lobster's Jell-O-like muscles are almost completely exposed. At this point it is almost totally defenseless. The lobster eats its old shell to absorb additional calcium and minerals stored in the old shell, then seeks out shelter while it waits several days for the new shell to harden. This is one of the most dangerous periods in a lobster's life.

Some scientists believe lobsters are one of a handful of species that do not die of old age. If they can survive predation, disease and entrapment, they can grow to truly monstrous proportions. The largest known lobster, caught in Nova Scotia in 1977, weighed 44 pounds and was estimated to be over 100 years old. In the early 1800s, before lobsters were commercially harvested, reports of four-foot lobsters weighing up to 50 pounds were not uncommon.

Lobster sex is particularly strange. Because a hard shell reduces access to the female's anatomy, lobsters have sex immediately after the female has molted. During courtship, an alpha male will wander around the ocean floor and evict several females from their shelters before returning to his own shelter. Interested females, who will only mate with the dominant alpha male, will wander over to the alpha male's shelter and pee inside. The alpha male, in turn, happily swirls the urine around himself. (As if this weren't strange enough, lobsters pee through an opening in their face.) Eventually the female moves in, sheds her shell, and the lobsters copulate. For the next week or so, as the female waits for her new shell to harden, she will stay in the male's shelter under his protection. When she leaves, a new female immediately takes her place.

Females can carry the male's sperm for several month before putting it to use, and they can even store some sperm for a second batch of eggs. Eggs develop inside the female before attaching themselves to the underside of her tail. Depending on the size of the female, her tail can carry anywhere between 5,000 and 100,000 eggs.

When the eggs finally hatch, tiny lobster larvae are dispersed into the ocean and float aimlessly wherever the currents take them. Only a few will survive this dangerous period—most will be eaten by predators. After molting for the fourth time in three weeks, the tiny, half-inch long lobsters settle to the ocean floor where they will spend the rest of their lives. Baby lobsters that settle on sandy bottoms are often eaten immediately by predators. Baby lobsters that settle on cobble-covered bottoms—of which there are plenty in the Gulf of Maine—often grow to adulthood.

Lobsters turn red when cooked, but their shell is a dark greenish-brown while they're still alive. A lobster's shell has multiple pigments, and all but the red pigment are destroyed when the lobster is cooked. In rare cases lobsters are born with a genetic mutation that only gives them a single pigment. Every few years, a lobstermen pulls up a blue or yellow lobster. In extremely rare cases, a lobster's coloration is split down the middle—half yellow, half blue.

ANATOMY OF A LOBSTER

Shredder Claw
This sharp, slender claw shreds the flesh of victims. It is composed of fast muscle fibers, which contract rapidly but tire easily.

Crusher Claw
This large, powerful claw is used to crush the shells of prey such as clams and mussels. It is composed of slow muscle fibers, which produce strong contractions of long duration.

Antennules
A lobster's antennules contain hundreds of chemical receptors that give lobsters an extraordinary sense of smell. Lobsters "sniff" by flicking the antennules up and down.

Carapace
This large backplate stretches from the eye socket to the top of the tail. Lobstermen measure the carapace to determine legal size.

Legs & Feet
Lobster have 10 legs, including the claws, which are covered with thousands of tiny hairs that sense touch and function as taste buds.

Antennae
These whip-like antennae are highly mobile, moving swiftly from side to side to detect motion. The two antennae can also sense bidirectional movement to determine water current direction.

Tail
A lobster's powerful tail can propel it backwards at speeds up to 25 miles per hour. Female lobsters carry eggs on the underside of their tails, and they have wider tails to accommodate more eggs. Large females can carry up to 100,000 eggs.

MAINE LOBSTERMEN

It's impossible to talk about coastal Maine without talking about lobstermen. Proud, tough and independent minded, they are the economic heart of small coastal communities and a vital cultural symbol of Maine. But it wasn't always this way.

Until the 1800s, lobster was largely considered a "garbage fish" barely worthy of harvesting. Lobster was collected close to shore by old men and young boys who lacked the strength to fish at sea. But as diners in New York discovered the taste of fresh lobster, demand increased. The 1840s saw the invention of the "lobster smack," a sailboat that could transport live lobsters over long distances, and canned lobster became big business in the 1870s. In the 1840s, there were only a few dozen lobstermen in Maine. By 1880, there were over 1,800.

When settlers first arrived in Maine, it was possible to gather large lobsters among the rocks at low tide. Eventually, however, harvesting reduced lobster populations along the shore, and wooden traps were invented and launched from rowboats. As the industry grew, rowboats were abandoned for sailboats—most notably Friendship Sloops built in Friendship, Maine—and in the 1930s and 1940s sailboats were abandoned for diesel-powered motorboats.

The next major change came in the 1970s when wooden traps were abandoned for more durable metal traps. Today lobster traps measure roughly 4 feet long and are divided into two chambers. The first chamber, the "kitchen," has twin, funnel-shaped openings where lobsters can enter the trap. From the kitchen a third funnel-shaped opening leads to the "parlor," where a bag of smelly bait has been placed. Once a lobster wanders into the parlor, it is effectively trapped.

Each trap is connected by rope to a floating buoy, which is painted with a color pattern unique to each lobsterman. After snagging the buoy, the lobsterman hauls the trap onboard with the aid of an electric motor, removes any lobsters, puts a fresh bag of bait in the trap, and then throws the trap overboard. Lobstermen are allowed a maximum of 800 traps.

According to the Gulf of Maine Research Institute, the average lobsterman is 50 years old and has been lobstering for 30 years. His boat is 32 feet long, 17 years old, and has a 260 horsepower engine. If he worked with a stern-

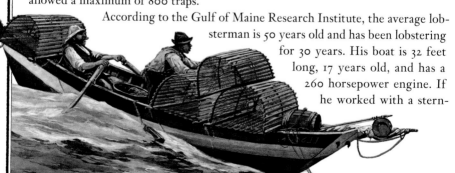

man (assistant), he landed over 24,000 pounds of lobster and earned an average of $25,000 after expenses. But depending on a lobsterman's work ethic, the wholesale price of lobster, and the price of gas, lobstermen can earn significantly more.

Today nearly every fisherman in Maine is a lobsterman. After other fish stocks collapsed in the early 1990s, lobstering took up the slack, and today there are roughly 6,000 lobstermen in Maine—up from 2,500 lobstermen in the 1970s. From an annual harvest of 20 million pounds in the 1980s, annual catches have skyrocketed to over 60 million pounds today. Amazingly, lobster populations in Maine appear to be stable. This is due, in large part, to the lobstermen themselves, who adhere to strict conservation measures that have allowed lobsters to flourish.

Lobster conservation laws were first enacted in the late 1800s, but back then they were largely ignored. When lobster catches collapsed in the 1920s, averaging five to seven million pounds, lobstermen finally embraced the conservation laws. Today all lobsters are measured, and lobstermen only keep lobsters with a carapace between 3¼ and 5 inches. All other lobsters are returned to the sea. This allows small lobsters to reach sexual maturity, and big lobsters (which produce exponentially more eggs) to reproduce. In addition, when lobstermen catch an egg-bearing female they cut a permanent V-notch on the tip of her tail. Once a female lobster acquires a V-notch, she can never be harvested.

Perhaps most fascinating, these conservation measures are almost entirely self-regulated. Lobstermen belong to unofficial "gangs" which work a specific harbor or territory. If anyone is caught breaking the rules, they face the wrath of the entire gang. Likewise, if a lobsterman encroaches on another gang's territory, subtle warning signals are sent. At first knots are tied on the offending lobsterman's buoy. If the violations continue, trap ropes are cut. And in severe cases, lobsterboats are vandalized. This social pressure, it turns out, is far more effective than government intervention, especially when there are only 32 wardens to patrol 2,500 miles of Maine coast. It also helps that lobstermen have good working relationships with government officials and a strong personal sense that the system works for them.

In recent years, the Maine lobster industry's unusual success has drawn the attention of prominent researchers. In 2009 the Nobel Prize in Economics was awarded to Elinor Ostrom (the first woman ever to win the prize) for her work on the management of common property by common ownership, which examined Maine lobstermen. Someday, the unorthodox solutions developed on the coast of Maine may help conserve other natural resources around the world.

WHALES

THE GULF OF MAINE'S cold, nutrient-rich water and shallow depth make it one of the most biologically productive marine habitats in the world. In the summer, when the nutrients are at their peak, hundreds of migrating whales arrive here to feed on the natural bounty. From 85-foot finback whales to 5-foot harbor porpoises, the variety of whales found in the Gulf of Maine is extraordinary.

Whales are warm-blooded mammals that breath air, have hair, and give birth to live young. Although mammals evolved roughly 200 million years ago, whales did not appear until roughly 50 million years ago. Around that time, a few land-dwelling mammals began spending more and more time in the ocean, and after several million years they evolved into purely marine animals—the ancestors of modern whales. Even today, whale fetuses develop a pair of rear legs that are genetic remnants of their land-dwelling ancestors. Although these tiny legs fail to fully develop, tiny "leg bones" are visible in the skeletons of many whales.

Whales are divided into two major categories: toothed whales and baleen whales. Toothed whales, such as sperm whales, have teeth in their mouths which they use to grind up fish and other prey. Baleen whales, such as humpbacks, have mouths filled with hundreds of fibrous, closely-spaced baleen plates. The baleen plates—made of keratin, the same substance found in human fingernails—allows whales to filter out plankton and fish from swallowed seawater. Although there are over 70 species of toothed whale and only 12 species of baleen whales, baleen whales are the most commonly spotted large whales in the Gulf of Maine.

Because whales are warm-blooded, they must maintain a constant body temperature of 98.6 °F, which can be difficult in frigid waters like the Gulf of Maine. To help retain warmth, whales have a thick layer of fat, called blubber, located just under their rubbery skin. In large baleen whales this layer of blubber can be up to two feet thick. But while the thick, oily blubber has helped whales survive the elements for millions of years, it nearly resulted in their extinction in modern times.

Three hundred years ago people relied on oil rendered from whale blubber to fuel their lamps and lubricate their machines. In the 1700s whales were aggressively hunted in New England waters, and by the early 1800s whale populations throughout the world were in steep decline. When petroleum was developed as a cheap alternative to whale oil in the late 1800s, the whale oil industry collapsed.

Several decades later, however, new motorized boats and exploding harpoons allowed whalers to hunt whale species that had previously been too fast to catch. At the same time, new chemical processes allowed whale oil to be rendered into margarine and soap. Blue whales and finback whales suffered devastating declines before a moratorium on commercial whaling was established in 1986. Today some whale populations are recovering, but many remain threatened due to deaths by fishing nets and accidental boat strikes.

ALLIED WHALE

For nearly 40 years, researchers at Allied Whale have been studying migrating whales and other marine mammals in the waters off Mount Desert Island. Founded in 1972 as a non-profit research arm of Bar Harbor's College of the Atlantic, Allied Whale pioneered the identification of humpback whales by studying their unique tail markings. Today they keep a database of over 25,000 whale photos to help track population and migration patterns. In addition, Allied Whale operates the most remote field research station on the eastern seaboard: Mount Desert Rock, a tiny island 20 miles south of Mount Desert Island (p.117). To find out more, visit the Bar Harbor Whale Museum (p.228), where all profits are donated to Allied Whale.

Humpback Whale *(Megaptera novaeangliae)*

Famous for their acrobatic displays and crooning songs, humpbacks can grow up to 60 feet long and weigh up to 45 tons. Over 10,000 humpbacks spend their summers feeding in the western North Atlantic, eating up to 3,000 pounds of fish and krill per day, and often doubling their weight by fall. After storing up enough fat to carry them through the winter, the whales migrate south to the Caribbean to breed and raise calves. During this time adults do not feed at all, but calves consume up to 100 gallons of mother's milk each day. An arch in the back gives the whale its common name, while the long flippers—the longest of any whale—give humpbacks their scientific name: *Megaptera novaeangliae*, "Big Wing of New England." (Humpbacks were first studied in New England.) Humpbacks are found throughout the world's oceans, and they have the longest migration of any animal—5,000 miles.

Northern Right Whale *(Eubalanea glacialis)*

The northern right whale is one of the rarest animals in the world with a population of less than 350 in the North Atlantic. Among the bulkiest of whales, they are slow moving giants that can weigh up to 100 tons, which made them the main target of whalers. Right whales—so named because they were the "right" whales to hunt—were nearly extinct by the 1900s. Although an international hunting ban was enacted in 1931, their populations have barely recovered since then. In the winter mothers and calves swim in the waters off northern Florida and Georgia. Right whales grow up to 60 feet long, and their heads are often covered in large skin growths called callosities, which are home to several species of whale lice.

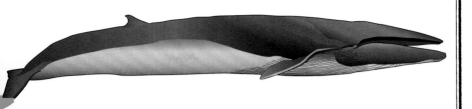

Finback Whale *(Balaenoptera physalus)*

Finbacks, the most commonly spotted whales off Mount Desert Island, are the second largest whales in the world after blue whales. Finbacks can grow up to 85 feet long and weigh up to 70 tons. They are named for a prominent dorsal fin located two-thirds of the way down the back. After coming to the surface for air, a finback will breath 5 to 15 times in a row, diving a short distance between breaths. Each breath raises their back and dorsal fin higher and higher out of the water. The final breath leads to a "terminal dive" where the finback arches its back five to six feet above water, then dives underwater for up to 15 minutes. During this time the finback can reach depths up to 750 feet. Finbacks return to the same feeding areas in the North Atlantic year after year, but where they mate and give birth remains unknown. There are an estimated 16,000 finback whales in the North Atlantic.

Minke Whale *(Balaenoptera acutorostrata)*

Minke whales are relatively small whales, growing up to 30 feet long and weighing up to 11 tons. Because of their size, they avoided the attention of whalers. Today they are the world's most common baleen whale with an estimated population of one million. Minke whales are found in all oceans of the world, but they prefer cold environments like the North Atlantic. Larger minke whales tend to migrate farther north in the summer than smaller minke whales, and adult females migrate farther north than males. In the Gulf of Maine, the majority of minke whales are smaller juveniles. Because they venture closer to shore than larger whales, minke whales are sometimes seen in harbors and bays.

Harbor Seals & Gray Seals

Harbor seals (*Phoca vitulina*) are often seen swimming in the waters off Mount Desert Island and basking on offshore ledges. They are 5–6 feet long, weigh up to 290 lbs., and come in a wide range of colors including black, gray, tan and white. Harbor seals have large, round eyes that give them superior vision in dark, murky water. But because they lack ducts to drain eye fluids, tears flow continuously down their eyes. They can swim up to 12 mph, dive up to 300 feet, and stay submerged for up to 28 minutes. While diving their heart rate slows from 120 beats/minute to six beats/minute to conserve oxygen.

Gray seals, which are significantly larger than harbor seals, have recently become much more common in Maine waters. They can grow up to 8 feet long and weigh up to 800 pounds. Gray seals are easily identified by their distinctive, horse-like face and prominent curved nose. (The gray seal's scientific name, *Halichoerus gryphus*, literally means "hook-nosed sea pig.")

In the late 1800s fishermen put a bounty of $1 per head on seals to reduce competition for fish. By the time the bounty was repealed in 1905, seals were nearly exterminated along much of the Maine coast. In 1972 the Marine Mammal Protection Act banned hunting of all marine mammals, and seal populations have slowly rebounded since then.

Peregrine Falcon *(Falco peregrinus)*

Peregrine falcons are birds of prey that can spot victims from thousands of feet above. Once a target is selected, a peregrine dives bombs it at speeds topping 100 mph. The collision creates an explosion of feathers, and victims that don't die upon impact have their necks broken by the peregrine's powerful beak. Peregrines are such successful strikers that they were used to kill Nazi carrier pigeons in World War II. By the early 1970s, however, the worldwide peregrine population had been reduced to less than 40 pairs due to hunting, habitat loss, and the effects of the pesticide DDT. To save the remaining birds, young peregrines were raised in captivity and released in the wild, including here in Acadia (p.150).

Bald Eagle *(Haliaeetus leucocephalus)*

Bald Eagles range over much of North America, but in Maine they are mostly found along the coast where they prey on seabirds. Although bald eagles range over a vast territory, most return to nest within 100 miles of where they were raised. Nests are reused each year and are added to annually—some can reach up to 10 feet across and weigh up to 2,000 pounds. Eagles can live up to 30 years, and their wingspan can top seven feet. The bird's scientific name means "white-headed sea eagle." By the 1960s there were fewer than 900 bald eagles in the lower 48 states. Today, following effective conservation programs, there are over 30,000.

Osprey *(Pandion haliaetus)*

Often spotted soaring over the ocean, ospreys fly high above the water looking for fish. When an osprey spots a fish near the surface, it swoops down and snatches it out of the water with powerful talons. Ospreys are amazingly effective hunters that can catch up to 80% of their prey. Occasionally they will catch two fish—one in each talon. Osprey wingspans can reach six feet across, and their nests, built out of sticks, can top 12 feet in height. Osprey are found on every continent except Antarctica. Ospreys that spend their summers on Mount Desert Island have been recorded as far away as Haiti and Honduras in the winter.

Puffin *(Fratercula arctica)*

Puffins spend most of their lives on the open ocean, returning to land only to raise chicks in the spring and summer. They are amazing swimmers that use their wings to "fly" underwater and their feet to steer. Puffins hunt small fish underwater and can carry an astounding 60 fish in their beak at one time. Puffins were over-hunted in Maine by early settlers, and by 1900 only one colony remained. In the 1970s puffin chicks from Newfoundland were reintroduced to a handful of offshore islands, and today there are several breeding colonies—including one on Petit Manan island near Schoodic Peninsula. The puffin's scientific name, *Fratercula arctica*, means "little friar of the north," a reference to its robe-like coloration.

Loon *(Gavia immer)*

Famous for their haunting call, loons are found on freshwater lakes in the summer and protected ocean bays in the winter. Loons are powerful swimmers, but famously clumsy on land. (The word "loon" is supposedly derived from the Scandinavian word *lom*, meaning clumsy person.) Their bright red eyes are capable of seeing at depths below 15 feet, and unlike most flying birds they have relatively solid bones that enable them to dive up to 150 feet. While underwater loons pursue fish and other prey with dagger-like bills. Chicks take to the water within hours of hatching, and occasionally they hitch a ride on their parents' backs.

Herring Gull *(Larus argentatus)*

Adult herring gulls are easily identified by their gray wings and black wing tips. Juveniles are often mottled brown. Gulls eat just about anything, including fish, shellfish, garbage, and baby seabirds. The red spot on a gull's yellow bill is a target for chicks, who peck at it to indicate hunger. If pecked, adults will regurgitate food into the chick's mouth. Although ubiquitous today, herring gull populations collapsed in the 1800s due to egg poaching, habitat disturbance, and hunters seeking feathers for the hat industry. Populations have since rebounded, and today there are over 200,000 herring gulls off the coast of Maine.

Common Eider Duck
(Somateria mollissima)

The common eider is the largest duck in the northern hemisphere and one of the most commonly spotted birds in the waters off Mount Desert Island. Males have dramatic black and white plumage with white cheeks and light green coloration on the back of the neck. Females are brown all over. Adult eiders feed primarily on shellfish, swallowing mussels and crabs whole. Eider stomachs are specially designed to crush shellfish and digest both the shell and its contents.

Female eiders are solely responsible for the incubation of the egg, which is kept warm with a layer of soft down plucked from the mother's breast. When young eiders hatch, they are immediately led to the shore to feed. But the journey is a treacherous one. Young eiders can be preyed upon by gulls, eagles, hawks and fish.

Although common today, Atlantic eiders faced extinction in the late 1800s. Back then eiders were aggressively hunted for their soft down, which was used in pillows and quilts. By the early 1900s there was only one breeding population in Maine. A harvesting ban was enacted to save the birds, and populations slowly recovered. Today eiders are one of the most numerous seabirds in Maine. They can sometimes be seen gathering in large "rafts" of several thousand birds on the open water.

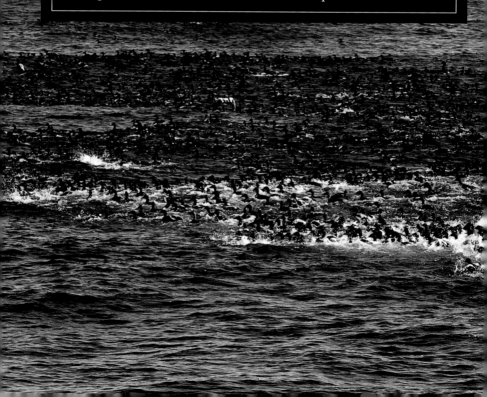

BEAVER

Castor canadensis

Beavers, the largest rodents in North America, are found in several ponds on Mount Desert Island. They use their large incisors to gnaw on tree trunks, then drag the toppled trees to streams to build dams. Beaver dams are built out of logs, sticks and rocks cemented together with mud. The resulting pond creates prime wetland habitat for beavers and many other animals. Once a dam is built, beavers construct a living space called a lodge by heaping together a separate pile of debris, then gnawing out a roomy chamber from the bottom up. Because beavers store food underwater, they require a deep pond that won't fully freeze in the winter, allowing them access to their food. Beavers have large, webbed hind feet to aid in swimming, and they use their long, flat tails as rudders while towing trees and branches in the water. On land, beavers use their tail to prop themselves up when gnawing on trees. The beaver's double fur coat, which is so thick that water never touches a beaver's skin, was prized by early trappers, and throughout the 1700s and 1800s beavers were hunted extensively. By 1900 beavers had been removed from much of their natural range, including Mount Desert Island. Protective laws and reintroduction programs were later enacted, and populations slowly recovered. Beavers were successfully reintroduced to Acadia in 1920.

U.S. RANGE

INFO

WEIGHT: 30 to 75 lbs.

LENGTH: 3.5 feet

LIFESPAN: 15 to 20 years

TRACKS:

BLACK BEAR

Ursus americanus

Black bears are the most common bear in North America with roughly 800,000 black bears in the U.S. and Canada. They can run up to 30 mph and search for food with a nose that is 100 times more powerful than a dog's. Most of their diet consists of berries, nuts and leaves, but bears will tear open rotting logs to eat ants, larvae and bugs. Black bears have a voracious appetite, often doubling their weight by winter to prepare for hibernation. But black bears are not true hibernators—they are simply too large to dissipate enough heat to enter true hibernation, which requires a body temperature near freezing. Rather, bears enter a deep sleep more properly described as "winter lethargy" where their body temperature stays relatively warm. Pregnant females wake in mid-winter to give birth, then fall back asleep while the seven-ounce newborns nestle in their mother's fur to stay warm. Cubs nurse for up to a year, and stay with their mother until about 1.5 years in age. Several individual black bears live and breed on Mount Desert Island, but they are rarely seen. In the fall of 2005, however, a black bear wandered into downtown Bar Harbor and spent an afternoon in a tree next to the Municipal Building.

U.S. RANGE

INFO

LENGTH: 5 feet

SHOULDER HEIGHT: 3 feet

WEIGHT: 250 to 350 lbs.

TRACKS:

MOOSE

Alces alces

Moose, the largest member of the deer family, are majestic animals that can weigh an astonishing 1,800 pounds. Despite their massive size they are surprisingly nimble—they can swim up to six miles per hour and run through forest up to 35 miles per hour. Moose are distinguished by the bull's massive antlers, which can stretch six feet across and weigh up to 50 pounds. A bull's antlers start growing in the spring and are shed by December. Antlers are used to mark territory, dig up plants from the bottom of ponds, and, most importantly, fight with other males. Moose require 50 to 60 pounds of vegetation daily. They feed by wrapping their thick, rubbery lips around a twig and, in a single motion, stripping away the leaves, bark and buds. Their name comes from the Algonquian *moosu*, which has been translated as "twig eater." Moose are relatively recent arrivals in North America—they are believed to have crossed the Bering land bridge from Siberia during the last Ice Age. Although common throughout most of Downeast Maine, they are rarely seen on Mount Desert Island. Occasionally, however, moose are spotted on Schoodic Peninsula or swimming among the islands of Blue Hill Bay.

U.S. RANGE

INFO

WEIGHT: up to 1,800 lbs.

HEIGHT: 7 feet

LIFESPAN: up to 20 years

TRACKS:

PORCUPINE

Erethizon dorsatum

Porcupines are slow, clumsy animals that achieve a maximum speed of two miles per hour. They wander from tree to tree in search of food, feeding upon twigs, leaves and bark. Among their favorite trees are hemlock and sugar maples. Lovers of salt, porcupines will also gnaw on the wooden handles of tools that have absorbed human sweat. Porcupines are famous for their quills, which are actually stiff, modified hairs. Adult porcupines have an astounding 30,000 quills, roughly 140 per square inch. Quills are used for protection, but contrary to popular belief porcupines cannot throw their quills. Rather, they lash out at enemies with their tails, where the quills are loosely attached. If the tail strikes an enemy, the quills detach and lodge themselves in the victim's skin. But porcupines are not aggressive, and if left alone they will not attack. Porcupines have quills all over their body except their face and underside. Not surprisingly, porcupine mating is a bit complicated. The female must relax her quills to avoid harming the male. Babies are born with soft quills to avoid injury to the mother, but the quills harden within a half an hour of birth. Indians considered porcupine meat a delicacy, and decorated baskets and canoes with porcupine quills.

U.S. RANGE

INFO

WEIGHT: 15 to 25 lbs.

LENGTH: 2 to 3 feet

LIFESPAN: up to 18 years

TRACKS:

RACCOON

Procyon lotor

Famous for the black "mask" that covers their face, raccoons are intelligent, crafty creatures. Their eyes are incredibly well adapted to darkness, allowing them to carry out mischievous deeds at night such as removing trash lids and prying open coolers to steal food. A common myth holds that raccoons always wash their food before they eat it, but these beady-eyed bandits are hardly that dignified. Raccoons eat just about anything they can get their hands on, clean or dirty, including frogs, birds, fruits, nuts, worms, slugs and garbage. They are especially ravenous in the fall, increasing their body fat up to 50 percent to prepare for the lean winter months. Although raccoons prefer wooded areas near streams, they have adapted remarkably well to urban environments, traveling along sewage pipes and living in attics and chimneys. Despite their cute and cuddly appearance, raccoons have a nasty disposition and a tendency to carry rabies, so they should never be approached. The name raccoon is supposedly derived from the Algonquian *arakunem*, which means "one that scratches with its hands." Other tribes have similar names for raccoons that refer to the animal's nimble hands.

U.S. RANGE

INFO

WEIGHT: 10 to 30 lbs.

LENGTH: 3 feet

LIFESPAN: up to 4 years

TRACKS:

RED FOX

Vulpes fulva

Sleek and swift, crafty and cunning, red foxes have captivated wildlife watchers throughout the world. Highly adaptable, their range includes North America, Europe, Asia, North Africa—even Iceland and Japan. Although a member of the dog family, foxes display many feline characteristics such as stalking, pouncing, and toying with wounded prey. They have elliptical cat-like eyes, with pupils that can shrink to a narrow slit, giving them exceptional vision in bright light. In addition, a reflective membrane at the back of the eye causes light to pass over the retina twice, giving them excellent vision at night. Their superior vision, combined with ears that are sensitive enough to hear mouse footsteps under snow and a sense of smell that is 100 times greater than that of humans, makes them highly skilled hunters. Foxes eat virtually anything they can catch, including grasshoppers, crickets, small birds, squirrels, rabbits and lizards. Mothers often bring partially dead animals back to the den for the pups to play with to sharpen their survival skills. While still less than a month old, pups fight among themselves to establish dominance. The more dominant pups are fed first by the parents.

U.S. RANGE

INFO

WEIGHT: 9 to 12 pounds

LENGTH: 3 feet

LIFESPAN: up to 4 years

TRACKS:

SNOWSHOE HARE

Lepus americanus

Snowshoe hares are masters of disguise. In the summer they sport a grayish brown coat that helps them blend in with grasses and shrubs. As winter approaches, shorter days trigger a biological response that turns their coat almost entirely white, providing excellent camouflage in the snow. Snowshoe hares are preyed upon by foxes, coyotes, owls and hawks. When the hare senses a predator, it freezes to avoid detection. If necessary it can flee at speeds up to 30 mph, hopping 12 feet in a single bound and making sharp zigzags to confuse predators. Snowshoe hares often spend their days sleeping in hidden locations, becoming active only at night or in the low light of dawn or dusk. They mate and give birth year-round. Females produce up to eight young per litter, up to four times per year. Young hares run within hours of birth. The populations of snowshoe hares are highly cyclical, becoming extremely plentiful every 10 years or so, then plummeting dramatically. The cause of this phenomenon is not fully understood. It may have to do with unsustainable population densities. Researchers have studied some areas that contain up to 10,000 snowshoe hares per square mile.

U.S. RANGE

INFO

LENGTH: 15 to 20 inches

WEIGHT: 2 to 3 lbs.

LIFESPAN: up to 4 years

TRACKS:

WHITE-TAILED DEER

Odocoileus virginianus

White-tailed deer are the most abundant large mammal in North America. Before Columbus, North America's white-tailed deer population may have numbered as high as 40 million, but by the mid-1800s hunting had reduced that number to roughly 1 million. Sportsmen, alarmed at the decline, pushed for wildlife management practices that allowed populations to bounce back. But ever since the near extermination of mountain lions and wolves, deer's natural predators, white-tailed deer have become dependent on humans to keep their population in check. Without adequate hunting, deer populations would explode to unsustainable levels. Bucks are prized for their antlers, which they use as weapons to determine dominance during breeding season (rut) in the fall. Bucks shed their antlers every winter and regrow them for the fall rut. Each spring, does usually give birth to twins, although in rare cases they give birth to triplets or quadruplets. Newborn deer are virtually defenseless. To avoid detection by predators, they have white spots on their back that help them blend in with the sun-dappled forest floor.

U.S. RANGE

INFO

WEIGHT: 150 to 250 lbs.

LIFESPAN: up to 4 years

POPULATION: 25 million

TRACKS:

Passamaquoddy Man

HISTORY

NOT LONG AFTER Ice Age glaciers retreated from New England, humans settled the land. Around 10,000 years ago, pre-Indian hunters arrived in Maine and scraped out a living on the tundra left in the glacier's wake. At the time, Ice Age creatures such as mammoths, mastodons and six-foot long beavers roamed the inland regions. The hunters chased game throughout the interior of the state, but it wasn't until about 5,000 years ago that the coast of Maine was settled. By that point temperatures had warmed, many Ice Age mammals had become extinct (most likely due to over hunting), and the modern ecology of Maine had started to take shape.

Maine's Indians are collectively known as the Wabanaki, a group that includes the Penobscot, Passamaquoddy, Micmac and Maliseet tribes. *Wabanaki*, loosely translated, means "People of the Dawn" due to Maine's eastern location—one of the first places in North America to see the rising sun. The Wabanaki were highly mobile, moving seasonally to take advantage of various plants and animals. They paddled birchbark canoes on rivers and lakes, and established temporary villages on the banks of rivers and along the coast.

Of the four Wabanaki tribes, the Penobscot and the Passamaquoddy are the two most closely associated with Mount Desert Island. They called the island *Pemetic*, "Mountain Range," and lived in seasonal camps in present-day Northeast Harbor and Bar Harbor, as well as on several offshore islands.

On Mount Desert Island the Wabanaki diet was rich in seafood. The men speared haddock and bass, harpooned seals and porpoises, and sometimes paddled over a mile offshore at night to hunt sturgeon by torchlight. Women collected clams, mussels and other shellfish near the shore. (The Wabanaki refer to Bar Harbor as *Manesayd'ik*, "The Clam-Gathering Place.") Seafood that was not immediately eaten was smoked and stored for winter use.

On land the Wabanaki supplemented their diet with nuts, berries and seabird eggs. They hunted moose and deer with arrows and spears, and trapped smaller animals such as beavers and otters. In winter the Wabanaki chased game on snowshoes, which allowed them to move quickly across deep snows that slowed down their prey. In spring they supplemented their diet with cultivated crops and bartered for food with neighboring Indian communities.

The Wabanaki lived in portable wigwam dwellings that could be easily assembled in a few hours. Three wooden poles formed a basic conical framework to which birch bark panels were lashed. In the winter, the birch bark was further insulated with deerskin. There was a central fire pit, as well as sleeping areas carpeted with fragrant balsam tips and soft animal hides. An overhead platform provided extra storage space for utensils, dried food and extra furs.

When European explorers first arrived in Maine in the early 1600s, there were an estimated 32,000 Wabanaki living in Maine and Canada (about 41 people per 100 square miles). European explorers were fascinated by the Wabanaki. As one visitor noted, "I should consider these Indians incomparably more fortunate than ourselves ... their lives are not vexed by a thousand annoyances ... They mutually aid one another in their needs with much charity and without selfseeking. There is a continual joy in their wigwams." Another observer claimed that the Wabanaki "start off to their different places with as much pleasure as if they were going on a stroll ... for their days are all nothing but pastime."

Physical differences were also noted. One early European explorer observed that the Wabanaki "have no beards, the men no more than the women ... They have often told me that at first we seemed to them very ugly with hair both upon our mouths and heads; but gradually they have become accustomed to it, and now we are beginning to look less deformed."

Although Europeans did not settle the Maine coast until the mid-1700s, European contact had an immediate impact on Wabanaki life. In the early 1600s a European fad for beaver-pelt hats decimated beaver populations in Europe, and trappers soon eyed North America's abundant beaver population. With demand running high, Indians like the Wabanaki traded pelts for metal tools, guns and alcohol. But as trading with Europeans increased, the Wabanaki began to abandon their traditional, self-sufficient lifestyle in favor of the international marketplace.

At the same time, newly introduced European diseases such as smallpox, cholera and influenza ravaged Wabanaki communities. These diseases had previously ravaged European populations several centuries earlier, but many of the survivors developed a crude immunity. North American Indians had no such immunity. In 1618 alone a massive plague killed nearly three-quarters of the native population of coastal Maine. Within a few decades, up to 90 percent of the Wabanaki population had perished. With their communities decimated, many of the remaining Wabanaki abandoned their traditional religious beliefs, and French missionaries converted many to Christianity.

By the late-1700s the Wabanaki population in Maine had fallen to roughly 1,200 individuals. At the same time, the white population in Maine jumped from 54,000 to 300,000 in a matter of decades. As a result, the remaining Wabanaki lost access to much of their traditional territory, including parts of Mount Desert Island. But much of the coast remained unoccupied, and for several decades the Wabanaki continued to spend part of the year near the ocean to fish, hunt and gather food along the shore.

EUROPEAN DISCOVERY

SOME HISTORIANS BELIEVE Vikings were the first Europeans to visit the coast of Maine. Others have speculated that European fisherman secretly fished Maine's waters long before Columbus set sail. (Some even believe that prior to 1492 Columbus overheard fisherman on the docks of Bristol, England discussing North America, thus inspiring his historic voyage.) But the first recorded voyage to Maine comes from Giovanni De Verrazano, an Italian navigator who led a French expedition to the New World in 1524.

By the time Verrazano set sail, Spain and Portugal had explored the New World from Florida to the tip of South America, and John Cabot had led an English expedition to Newfoundland. But much of North America remained a mystery. Searching for a northern passage to Asia, Verrazano landed at present-day North Carolina and named it "Archadia" based on a mythical landscape described by the Greek poet Virgil. He then sailed north to explore the unknown coast.

When Verrazano reached Maine, he encountered the Wabanaki, whom he described as "of such crudity and evil manners, so barbarous, that despite all the signs we could make, we could never converse with them." As Verrazano's boat approached the shore, the Wabanaki yelled and shot arrows at them. They then indicated their desire to trade with the Europeans for metal tools—albeit with the aide of a basket on a line shuttled safely between the ship and the shore. When Verrazano's ship departed, the Wabanaki sent them off by "exhibiting their bare behinds." Verrazano returned the favor by naming the Maine coast *Terra Onde di Mala Gente*, "Land of Bad People."

The Wabanaki's less than hospitable "bon voyage" to Verrazano and their desire to trade for metal tools indicate that they had encountered Europeans before. But Verrazano was the first to officially map the region. Included on his map was a spot near Mount Desert Island mysteriously labeled "Oranbega."

Despite Verrazano's successful exploration, no permanent settlement was attempted in New England for almost a century. Europe, preoccupied with wars at home and the plunder of Central and South America to the south, paid little attention to chilly, remote New England. Although the rich waters off the coast of Maine were filled with fishermen by the late 1500s, they did little more than set up seasonal camps on offshore islands.

Before long, however, rumors of a fantastic city of gold located somewhere in Maine began to spread through Europe. The rumor is believed to have originated from a group of English sailors who were stranded in Mexico in 1567 and spent the next three years traveling on foot to New Brunswick, Canada. From there they hopped a fishing boat back to England and immediately hit the pubs, telling drunken stories of a fabulous city of gold located somewhere in Maine. They called the city "Norumbega"—a name strikingly similar to the "Oranbega" found on Verrazano's map.

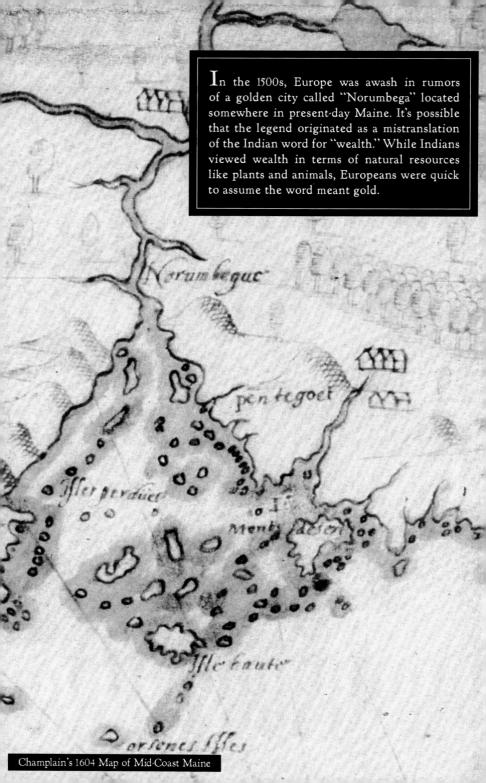

In the 1500s, Europe was awash in rumors of a golden city called "Norumbega" located somewhere in present-day Maine. It's possible that the legend originated as a mistranslation of the Indian word for "wealth." While Indians viewed wealth in terms of natural resources like plants and animals, Europeans were quick to assume the word meant gold.

Champlain's 1604 Map of Mid-Coast Maine

In the mid-1500s, the idea of a golden city in Maine would not have seemed terribly farfetched. Spain had hauled away enormous quantities of gold from the Aztecs and Incas, and it seemed only logical that more riches lay awaiting discovery in the New World. In 1579 and 1580, England sent two expeditions to midcoast Maine to search for Norumbega. Although the expeditions failed to find the golden city, the British officially named the entire region "Norumbega." (In 1606 the name Norumbega was changed to "Virginia," and fourteen years later Virginia was changed to "New England.")

But England was not the only country with an eye on the region—and dreams of easy riches were not so quickly forgotten. In 1603, seventeen years before the Pilgrims landed at Plymouth Rock, France sent an expedition to North America led by Samuel Champlain. After landing at the mouth of the St. Croix River in Canada, Champlain sailed south to explore the coast of Maine. When he spotted the bald peaks of Mount Desert Island, he noted in his log:

"The island is very high and notched in places, so that there is the appearance to one at sea, as of seven or eight mountains extending along near each other. The summit of most of them is destitute of trees, as there are only rocks on them. The slopes are covered with pines, firs, and birches. I named it *L'isle des Monts-déserts* [Island of Barren Mountains]."

Although earlier explorers had noticed the island before, Champlain was the first to give it a name. He was also the first to note that Mount Desert is, in fact, an island—previous maps had shown it connected to the mainland.

Continuing on, Champlain sailed up the Penobscot River, which empties into the Atlantic southwest of Mount Desert Island. If Norumbega existed, he hoped to find it there. Champlain made his way as far as present-day Bangor where he found, to his dismay, nothing more than a simple Indian village. Frustrated, he concluded that the city of Norumbega was a myth. He did point out, however, that the region as a whole was "marvelous to behold."

By the time of Champlain's voyage, Verrazano's name for North Carolina, Archadia, had slowly migrated north on French maps. As Verrazano's map was drawn and re-drawn by countless map makers, Archadia became "L'Acadie" and began to refer to the region between Philadelphia and Montreal—a region that would soon become a major point of contention between the English and the French.

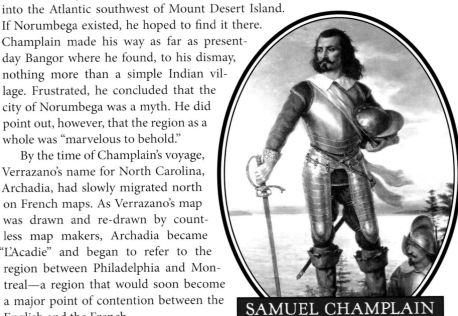

SAMUEL CHAMPLAIN

THE FRENCH JESUITS

LTHOUGH THERE WAS no gold in Maine, the region was overflowing with natural resources. "The aboundance of Sea-Fish," wrote one early fisherman, "are almost beyond beleeving." Cod grew up to six feet in length and could be gathered by simply dropping a bucket into the water. Sturgeons were so numerous near the shore that they were considered a navigational hazard. The natural bounty was all the more dramatic compared with Europe's own depleted resources. And the items that Europe needed most—timber, cod, beaver, and sassafras (mistakenly thought to cure syphilis)—were among the most abundant in New England. For over a century Europe had virtually ignored the region. But once New England's natural resources were recognized, it began to look a lot more promising.

By the time of Champlain's voyage, both England and France claimed that *they* were the rightful owner of North America. But with no English settlements in the New World, and only a handful of French settlements in Canada, there were no actual conflicts over the land. Then, in 1607, England established a permanent settlement at Jamestown, Virginia. In response, France's Louis XIII granted North America to French noblewoman Antoinette de Pons, Marquise de Guercheville, who proposed a Jesuit mission on the coast of Maine.

In May of 1613, two Jesuits and 48 settlers set sail from France, hoping to establish a mission along the Penobscot River. As they neared the coast of Maine, they became surrounded by a thick fog. Unable to see more than a few feet ahead, the Jesuits grew terrified. If their ship ran aground it could easily sink, and they would be stranded with no supplies. Poor winds prevented the boat from retreating to deeper water, and the helpless French settlers simply huddled together and prayed. For two days their ship drifted aimlessly through the fog. When the fog finally lifted, they found themselves staring at Mount Desert Island.

Overjoyed, the settlers rowed to shore and raised a cross. Not long after they landed, they were approached by a group of Wabanaki Indians who introduced themselves and encouraged the Frenchmen to stay on the island—presumably to benefit from the lucrative fur trade. But the Jesuits insisted that they would continue to the Penobscot River. The Wabanaki then informed them that their leader, Sagamore Asticou, was mortally ill and wished to be baptized before he died. Eager to save a soul, the Jesuits climbed into the Indians' canoes and were paddled to the southern end of the island.

When the Jesuits met Asticou, they found him suffering from no more than a common cold. Some historians have since speculated that Asticou simply faked sickness to draw the Jesuits near and convince them to stay. If that was the case, it worked. Asticou was baptized and the Jesuits established a small settlement named Saint Sauveur, "Holy Savior," just north of present-day Southwest Harbor.

Unfortunately for the French, English settlers in Jamestown, Virginia caught wind of their settlement plans, and a 14-gun warship was dispatched to deal with the intruders. When the warship's captain, Samuel Argall, reached Penobscot Bay, he encountered a group of Wabanaki fishing among the offshore islands. The Indians, assuming the white men were friends of the French, tipped them off to the Jesuit's settlement. By the time they realized their mistake, it was too late. Argall's ship sailed toward Mount Desert Island ready to attack.

The French, caught totally by surprise, put up a weak fight, firing off only a single round before their settlement was laid to waste. Argall allowed 14 Frenchmen to flee to Nova Scotia in an open boat, but the rest were taken to Jamestown as prisoners. When they arrived in Jamestown, the Governor of the colony threatened to hang the prisoners, but ultimately they were sent back to France.

The battle on Mount Desert Island was one of the first skirmishes between the English and the French in North America. But it would hardly be the last. For the next 150 years the two countries battled over the region, and Mount Desert Island became a virtual no man's land.

The Original Cadillac

In 1688 a young French lawyer named Antoine Laumet was granted 100,000 acres along the coast of Maine by the King of France. Undaunted by the violent land disputes in the region, the ambitious Laumet sailed to Mount Desert Island to oversee his new domain. Upon arriving in the New World, he changed his name to the noble sounding—yet completely fabricated—"*Antoine de La Mothe, Sieur de Cadillac*" and created a noble-looking coat of arms to complement his new name. But desolate Mount Desert Island offered little in the way of social mobility, and Cadillac headed west after only one summer. He later founded Detroit, Michigan, and today a modernized version of his fake coat of arms still graces the hood ornaments of Cadillac automobiles.

In 1786 Cadillac's granddaughter, Maria Teresa de Gregoire, contacted American authorities and claimed that she was the rightful owner of Mount Desert Island. Although her claim was legally dubious, the newly independent American government granted her the eastern half of the island as a show of goodwill toward the French. De Gregoire and her husband then moved to the island and started a real-estate company, selling land at $5.00 dollars per 100 acres. Today, there are only two places in the United States where real estate titles can be traced back to the King of France: Louisiana and Mount Desert Island.

SETTLEMENT BEGINS

NGOING BATTLES BETWEEN England and France kept many would-be settlers out of Maine until the late 1700s. During this time Mount Desert Island was used primarily as a navigational tool (on clear days its mountains can be seen up to 60 miles at sea). As one Englishman put it, the region north of the Penobscot River was "a Countrey rather to affright then delight one, and how to describe a more plaine spectacle of desolation, or more barren, I know not." But shortly before the 1763 Treaty of Paris, which granted England control of New England, Mount Desert Island received its first permanent settlers.

In 1761, 22-year-old Abraham Somes sailed north from Gloucester, Massachusetts, to Mount Desert Island and settled the town of "Betwixt the Hills" (later named Somesville). At the time, Mount Desert Island was owned by Francis Bernard, the royal governor of the Province of Massachusetts. Following the Revolutionary War, however, Bernard fled to England and the Americans confiscated his land. Bernard's son, who had sided with the Americans, ultimately petitioned the new government for his father's land, and being a good patriot he was granted it. But shortly after the transaction he sold the land and hightailed it back to England to join his father.

By the late 1700s, fertile land near the coast was in short supply in southern New England, and ambitious settlers began heading north to the undeveloped harbors in Maine. Before long, Mount Desert Island was growing at a healthy clip. Initial development took place in Somesville, but settlement soon spread throughout the island. In 1796 the town of Eden (later named Bar Harbor) was incorporated. Fishing, shipbuilding and lumbering were the primary occupations of the island's residents, who soon numbered several thousand, and for the most part they led peaceful, industrious lives. As one observer noted, "The women do the most of what there is in the way of farming, while the men, from early boyhood, are upon or in the water, chiefly as fishermen, but always as sailors, and unquestionably the best sailors in the world."

The island's economy revolved around the sea, and each day hundreds of sailboats could be seen plying the waters offshore. Local sailors shipped goods around the world, and many knew the coastlines of Europe and South America as well as they knew the coast of Maine. But sailing and fishing were rugged occupations. Men spent up to eight months of the year at sea, leaving their wives and children to fend for themselves at home.

Although Mount Desert Island continued to grow through the mid-1800s, access to the island from southern New England remained challenging. The journey was a multi-day affair that required a train ride to Portland, a steamboat cruise to Castine, and a schooner trip to Mount Desert Island. As a result, few outsiders knew much about this remote, beautiful island. But following the arrival of a handful of landscape painters from New York, all that was about to change.

Lobstermen, 1800s

Fitz Hugh Lane, *Entrance of Somes Sound from Southwest Harbor*, 1852

BOOM to BUST
Coastal Maine in the 1800s

As the Industrial Revolution swept across America in the 1800s, demand for natural resources boomed. And everything that America needed—fish for food, lumber for ships, granite for construction—Maine had in abundance. In an era when virtually everything was transported by ship, Maine also boasted the finest coast in the land, teeming with sheltered, deep-water harbors and thousands of offshore islands. After plodding along for centuries as an economic backwater, Maine had finally hit the jackpot.

Fishing had always been big business in Maine, and the fishing industry revolved around cod, which were easily caught, cured and transported. As American and European populations grew, demand for dried cod skyrocketed and fishing villages flourished on Maine's offshore islands. At the same time island forests were cut down for fuel, building material and farmland. After forests along the coast had been plundered, lumber barrens turned their eyes to the vast interior forests. By 1880, nearly half of Maine's forests had been cleared.

Back on the denuded coastal islands, entrepreneurs began quarrying the abundant granite. In those days granite was one of the most durable building materials, and because Maine islands were located alongside popular shipping routes, transportation was easy. On Mount Desert Island, Hall Quarry churned out enough granite to fill 10 to 15 schooners *each day*, some of which was used to build the Library of Congress.

Even the ice was valuable. In winter, huge blocks of ice were carved from rivers and ponds, covered in sawdust, and shipped around the world. From Bourbon Street to Bombay, Maine ice was considered a delicacy.

It seemed as if everything in Maine turned to gold. But a few decades after the Industrial Revolution showered Maine with easy riches, it took them away just as quickly. It started with the railroads, which opened up the vast virgin forests west of the Appalachian Mountains and permanently reduced America's reliance on coastal shipping routes. Maine's offshore islands, previously the best places to live and work, became the worst places to live and work. Coastal commerce collapsed, and hundreds of islands were abandoned.

At the same time, many independent fisherman found they couldn't afford new, expensive fishing technologies. Maine's fishing fleet, once the nation's largest, shrank by over 70%. When reinforced concrete was introduced, the granite industry collapsed. And when mechanical refrigeration became widespread, demand for Maine ice vanished. As the decades wore on, coastal Maine watched its once vibrant economy slowly decline. It wasn't long before people turned to the only lucrative industry that was left: tourism.

LIGHTHOUSES

Before the advent of trains and planes, the world relied on ships to transport nearly all commercial goods. And in the days before radar and GPS, ships depended upon lighthouses to guide them through dark and stormy conditions. Due to the craggy, treacherous nature of the Maine coast, 68 lighthouses were constructed here. By the late 1800s, it was possible to sail from one end of the state to the other and always be within sight of a lighthouse beacon. The earliest beacons were lit with whale oil and attended to by a keeper who lived at the lighthouse full time. Keepers, and their families, lived on remote islands for months or years at a time. Infrequent supply ships provided their only link to the mainland. By the late 1970s, however, every lighthouse had been automated, and lighthouse keepers were no longer necessary.

There's only one lighthouse on Mount Desert Island, Bass Harbor (p.266), but there are several others nearby. The oldest, Petit Manan (right), was built in 1828. At 96-feet, it's the second-tallest lighthouse in Maine. Other lights include Bear Island (p.248), Egg Rock (p.147), Baker Island (p.273), Winter Harbor (p.212), Hockamock Head (p.281), and Isle au Haut (p.217).

Mount Desert Rock Lighthouse

Although seldom seen by visitors, "The Rock" is one of the most famous lighthouses in America due to its remote location (20 miles south of Mount Desert Island), the island's exceptionally small size (1.5 acres), and the island's maximum height (15 feet above sea level). Originally built in 1830, the lighthouse was later fortified with granite walls four feet thick to withstand pounding waves. During particularly fierce storms, keepers would take shelter in the tower. In the 1880s three keepers and their families lived here, and a teacher would come during the summer to teach the children. One keeper's family didn't visit the mainland for eight years. The last full-time keepers left in 1977, and today the lighthouse is used as a whale research station by Allied Whale.

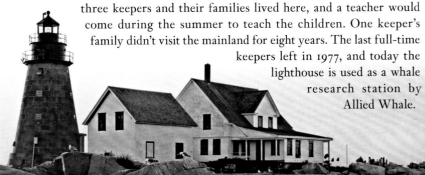

THE HUDSON SCHOOL PAINTERS

IN THE MID-1800s, American cities faced immense growing pains. Overpopulation and the effects of the Industrial Revolution had transformed previously habitable cities such as Boston, New York and Philadelphia into filthy, urban nightmares. Indoor plumbing had not yet been invented, and trash and human waste were left in the street to rot.

It's not surprising that during this time the art world experienced an overwhelming demand for landscape paintings. City dwellers, disgusted with the stink and grime of urban life, were desperate for wholesome scenes of unspoiled nature—hung conveniently on their townhouse walls. At the same time, railroads were creating an entirely new middle-class industry: tourism, which further fueled the demand for paintings of scenic destinations.

One of the first artists to visit Mount Desert Island was Thomas Doughty, who diligently worked his way up the coast in the early 1830s, booking passages on small sailing vessels. Doughty's paintings were later exhibited in New York, where they received moderate acclaim. They also caught the eye of his student, Thomas Cole, who was maturing into one of America's leading landscape artists.

In 1844 Cole traveled to Mount Desert Island with fellow artist Henry Cheever Pratt. The pair boarded at a farm near Schooner Head and painted dramatic scenes of Sand Beach, Otter Cliffs and Frenchman Bay. Cole was in awe of the rugged, coastal scenery. His diary from the trip includes passages describing "threatening crags, and dark caverns in which the sea thunders" and "a range of mountains of beautiful aerial hues."

When Cole's work was exhibited in New York the following summer, it opened to mixed, but predominantly negative, reviews. One critic chided Cole for painting red rocks, noting "the rocks are of a kind that no geologist would find a name for; the whole coast of Maine is lined with rocks nearly black in color." (In fact, the rocks on Mount Desert Island *do* have a reddish hue.) Another critic complained that "the ocean appears like a vast cabbage garden."

Despite the poor reviews, Cole's paintings were a hit with the public. And several years later Cole's aspiring young student, Frederic Church, set off to create his own paintings of Mount Desert Island. Only 24 years old, Church was considered something of a prodigy. He spent his days exploring the island's rugged terrain and produced a series of dramatic paintings that were received the following year with enormous success.

In the days before television or photography, landscape paintings offered a rare glimpse of exotic destinations, and landscape painters were often treated like modern-day rock stars. Church's stunning depictions of Mount Desert Island created a public frenzy. Thousands of people lined up outside galleries in New York to view his work, and other painters rushed to follow in his footsteps. Suddenly, Mount Desert Island found itself thrust into the national spotlight.

the Hudson River School

FREDERIC CHURCH

The painters of the Hudson River School not only introduced Mount Desert Island to the masses in the 1800s but also helped launch the American conservation movement. Two hundred years earlier, when the Puritans first arrived in New England, wilderness was viewed as a sinister, dangerous place—and back then it often was. The Puritans believed it was their moral duty to tame the wild land so religious communities could flourish. But even after the landscape had been tamed, their harsh view of nature persisted, and generations of Americans grew up viewing the frontier as an obstacle to be conquered. But as more and more pristine wilderness disappeared, a backlash developed.

Leading the charge were landscape painters such as Frederic Church and Thomas Cole, members of the Hudson River School of Art (which was not an actual school but an artistic movement). Cole rallied against the "apathy with which the beauties of external nature are regarded by the great mass, even of our refined community." Another artist declared, "Yankee enterprise has little sympathy with the picturesque, and it behooves our artists to rescue from its grasp the little that is left before it is for ever too late."

Artists of the Hudson School painted breathtaking scenes of the American wilderness that ignited the passions of the American public. They also used subtle visual techniques to convey their belief that wilderness was an extension *of* God, not an obstacle to His progress. One of their favorite tricks was to hide human features in the contours of rocks. This not only turned picture viewing into a kind of game, but also established a direct link between man and nature—and by extension God.

By portraying the American wilderness as a welcoming, spiritual destination, the Hudson School hoped to dispel the notion that nature was an obstacle. They also wanted to prove that the American landscape was just as beautiful as Europe (and possibly more so), creating a much needed sense of national pride for the young democracy. On both counts, they succeeded. Hudson School exhibitions drew huge crowds and lured thousands of tourists to pristine American destinations such as Mount Desert Island.

"The ladies wear wide-brimmed hats and picturesque costumes ... cut short above the feet and ankles, which, in turn, are incased in stout walking shoes. The gentlemen appear in warm, rough clothing, which will stand the wear and tear of a tramp over the rocks."

—*Harper's Magazine*, 1872

THE RUSTICATORS

CHURCH'S PAINTINGS GENERATED a flurry of interest in Mount Desert Island, and before long both artists and tourists were making the multi-day journey to see the island firsthand. In the summer of 1855, Church returned to Mount Desert Island with 26 friends, a group that included artists, writers, businessmen and their families. The group stayed at a Somesville tavern and spent their days hiking, fishing, sailing, picnicking and otherwise thoroughly enjoying themselves.

Although artists like Church were present, the excursion was first and foremost a social expedition. What little drawing was done generally consisted of humorous sketches mocking one another. At the end of their month-long stay, the group threw a large party. They invited dozens of locals and imported a piano, the island's first, specifically for the event. Church held forth at the piano, indulging in his "perfectly inexhaustible" capacity for entertainment late into the night.

What seemed like nothing more than a deliriously satisfying summer actually set the tone for the first wave of visitors to Mount Desert Island. Later named "Rusticators," these early tourists—for the most part artists, professors and other intellectuals with leisure time on their hands—came to experience the simple outdoor pleasures of rugged coastal life.

Rusticators required no fancy accommodations. They often rented out attic space from locals and paid for an extra spot at the family's dinner table. Locals, eager for some extra cash, were more than happy to accommodate the easy-to-please visitors, creating a wonderfully symbiotic relationship. An 1872 travel article in *Harper's Magazine* summed up the rusticator's lifestyle: "Now, most of the visitors to Mount Desert, even the prosaic folk, go prepared to enjoy the picturesque, the beautiful, the sublime."

Another article that year stated that "During the day parties of several persons, ladies and gentlemen, start off on a walking expedition of five, ten, and fifteen miles to one or another of the many objects of interest on the sea-shore or up the mountains. There is a vigorous, sensible, healthy feeling in all they do, and not a bit of that overdressed, pretentious, nonsensical, unhealthy sentimentality which may be found at other places."

But changes to the rusticator lifestyle were already under way. Several years earlier a New York journalist named Robert Carter had chartered a fishing sloop in Boston and taken a pleasure cruise to Mount Desert Island. At the time, there were no summer homes on the island and only two small inns. Carter reported that "of late years [Mount Desert Island] has become attractive to artists and summer loungers, but it needs the hand of cultivated taste." Although he could hardly have imagined it at the time, the arrival of a "cultivated hand" was not far away, and it would forever change the character of the island.

THE COTTAGERS

AS STORIES, ARTWORK, and magazine articles about Mount Desert Island continued to spread, interest in the island soared. But tourism was limited by the physical challenge of actually getting there. Few would-be tourists had the time, money or patience required for the multi-day journey. Then, in 1868, direct steamboat service was started between Boston and Mount Desert Island. A steamboat route drastically reduced the time it took to get to the island. It also dramatically increased the reliability of the voyage because travelers were no longer at the mercy of the wind. Within a few years, Mount Desert Island had become a major tourist destination.

Between 1868 and 1882, at least one hotel was built or thoroughly expanded on the island each year. The largest, Rodick House in Bar Harbor, contained over 400 rooms and was the largest hotel in Maine. Locals welcomed the flood of cash, but some were left feeling a bit perplexed. When one visitor told a local innkeeper that "It's the scenery we wish to see," the innkeeper replied, "Yes, I know, it's what them artist men come here for. But what it amounts to, after all their squattin' and fussin', I don't know."

In 1882 luxuries such as electricity and telephones arrived on Mount Desert Island, followed two years later by train service from Boston to Hancock Point, which was a short ferry ride away from Bar Harbor. The new train service cut travel time to Mount Desert Island down to a single day. The result was predictable: the number of summer visitors quadrupled.

The tourist explosion quickly changed the face of Bar Harbor. As more and more wealthy visitors arrived, upscale development proceeded at a breakneck pace. Luxury hotels sprouted on Bar Harbor farmland, and quaint general stores were replaced with boutiques showcasing the latest Parisian fashions.

An 1886 article in *Harper's* neatly summed up the situation: "For many years [Bar Harbor] had been frequented by people who have more fondness for nature than they have money, and who were willing to put up with wretched accommodations, and enjoyed a wild sort of 'roughing it.' But some society people in New York, who have the reputation of setting the mode, chanced to go there; they declared in favor of it; and instantly, by an occult law which governs fashionable life, Bar Harbor became the fashion."

The writer went on to describe a typical day at Rodick House: "The first confused impression was of a bewildering number of slim, pretty girls, nonchalant young fellows in lawn-tennis suits, and indefinite opportunities in the halls and parlors and wide piazzas for promenades and flirtations ... The big office is a sort of assembly room, where new arrivals are scanned and discovered, and it is unblushingly called the 'fish-pond' by the young ladies who daily angle there."

Hoping to distance themselves from hotel life, which was becoming increasingly less exclusive, the wealthiest visitors built giant mansions along the shore. So as not to appear pretentious, they referred to their mansions as "cottages." The name fooled no one, however, and before long the social epicenter had shifted from hotel lounges to private dinner parties. The wealthiest families in America all added Bar Harbor "cottages" to their portfolio of homes, and the arrival of these families firmly cemented Bar Harbor's reputation as one of the most exclusive summer destinations in America.

By 1896 there were nearly 200 mansions in Bar Harbor, and the tone of the town had completely changed. As longtime summer resident Edward Godkin put it, "The Cottager has become to the boarder what the red [squirrel] is to the gray, a ruthless invader and exterminator ... caste has been established ... the community is now divided into two classes, one of which looks down on the other."

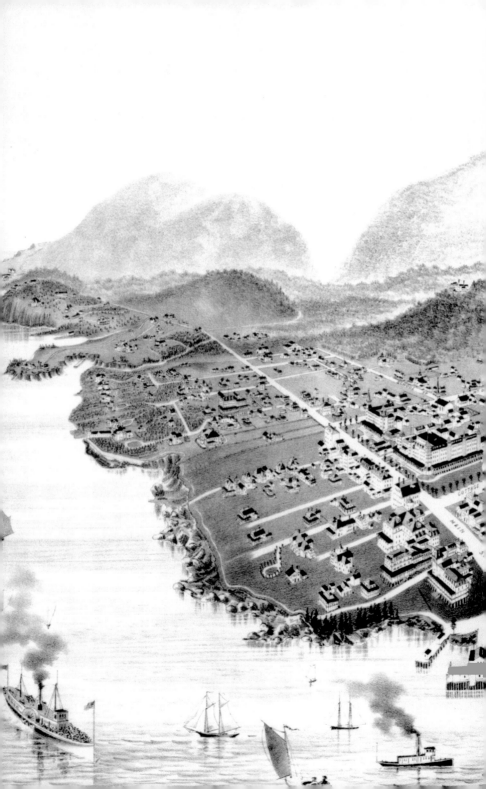

WEST ST.

Bar Harbor, late 1800s

Lost "Cottages" of
BAR HARBOR

WINGWOOD

WINGWOOD WAS THE most extraordinary summer cottage in Bar Harbor. It belonged to Edward T. Stotesbury, who grew up poor in Philadelphia, started working at age 12, and eventually became a senior partner at J.P. Morgan & Company. In 1925, flush with cash, Stotesbury purchased a large mansion in Bar Harbor. His wife Eva took one look at the new property, hired an architect, and ultimately spent over 1 million dollars remodeling the house. When the remodeling was complete, Wingwood boasted 80 rooms, 26 hand-carved marble fireplaces, 52 telephone lines, and a 30-room servants' wing. Some of Wingwood's bathrooms (28 total) featured gold fixtures, which Eva claimed were "economical" because "they saved polishing." For Edward, it was all a bit much. He once remarked to his gardener that he would have been content with a small cottage and a supper of beans. Instead, his meals were served on one of two 1,200 piece dining sets. Eva's spending habits were legendary. She hired gardeners to move plants around Wingwood's grounds on a weekly basis, and she employed a full-time fashion designer and "costume secretary." At one point Eva organized a $500,000 alligator safari to gather leather for a set of matching luggage. Following her death in 1946, Eva was remembered fondly as an exemplary hostess, one who "made every guest feel as if he or she were the only one invited." After the death of the Stotesburys, Wingwood fell into disrepair. It was ultimately demolished in 1953.

CHATWOLD

CHATWOLD WAS THE summer home of famed millionaire Joseph Pulitzer, by far the strangest cottager in Bar Harbor. After earning a fortune in the newspaper business—where he introduced such revolutionary concepts as the daily sports page and the color comic strip—Pulitzer added Chatwold to his collection of mansions in New York, Georgia and the French Riviera. His idiosyncrasies were legendary. Pathologically sensitive to noise, the sound of a nut cracking is said to have made him wince. When Pulitzer stayed in hotels he required the rooms above, below, and on either side of him to be kept vacant. To combat the irritating sounds of everyday life, Pulitzer spent $100,000 constructing the "Tower of Silence"—a massive granite structure on the right side of Chatwold that was designed to be 100 percent soundproof. The mansion also boasted the first heated swimming pool in Bar Harbor and a master bedroom that rotated on ball bearings.

Despite Pulitzer's legendary aversion to noise, he required a servant read him to sleep each night—and continue reading, in monotone, for at least two hours after he had fallen asleep. Legend has it he would awake at the slightest change in pitch. Pulitzer also spent at least 12 hours a day in bed, dictating letters to his secretaries in a self-devised code that contained over 20,000 names and terms; Pulitzer was "Andes," Theodore Roosevelt was "Glutinous," and so on. Chatwold was ultimately demolished in 1945, several decades after Pulitzer's death.

JOSEPH PULITZER

ACADIA NATIONAL PARK

BY THE TURN of the century, train service to Mount Desert Island had improved to the point where New Yorkers could hop a train in the morning and arrive in Bar Harbor by evening. As more and more tourists flooded the island, some citizens grew alarmed at the speed of development taking place. Speculators were snatching up real estate, and the lumber industry, equipped with modern machinery, was eyeing the island's vast untouched forests.

Among the citizens most alarmed was former Harvard president and longtime summer visitor Charles Eliot. With the help of his friend, wealthy island resident Charles Dorr, the two men organized a group of private citizens dedicated to preserving Mount Desert Island for future generations. As savvy as they were civic minded, the Hancock County Trustees of Public Reservations (as they later came to be called) obtained a tax-exempt charter and quickly set to work purchasing land. Dorr enthusiastically took charge and acquired Eagle Lake, Cadillac Mountain, Otter Cliffs and Sieur de Monts Spring—over 6,000 acres.

Things were going well until 1913, when the Maine Legislature, under pressure from a variety of sources, attempted to revoke the Trustee's tax-exempt charter. Worried that the charter might ultimately be dissolved, Dorr suggested that the Trustees donate their land to the federal government. This was easier said than done. More government land meant more government spending, and Dorr was dispatched to Washington to convince lawmakers that land preservation on Mount Desert Island was worth the money.

Using his considerable wealth and influence, Dorr pulled strings and cashed in on personal favors to arrange a meeting with President Woodrow Wilson. He also convinced the editors at National Geographic to publish an article about Mount Desert Island that generated tremendous public support for the cause. Two years later, a National Monument was created by Presidential Proclamation. Dorr's next move was to elevate the monument to national park status, which required an act of Congress. Despite the government's preoccupation with World War I, Dorr was able to gather the Congressional support he needed, and on February 26, 1919 Lafayette National Park was created. (The name Lafayette was chosen to reflect America's pro-French sentiment in the wake of the war.) Lafayette was the first national park established east of the Mississippi, and the first national park donated entirely from privately owned land.

Dorr became the park's first superintendent—at a salary of $1.00 per year—and he worked hard to expand Lafayette's holdings. In the late 1920s, a family of Anglophiles donated Schoodic Peninsula with the stipulation that the name of the park be changed to something less French. And so, in 1929, Lafayette National Park became Acadia National Park. (Ironically, Acadia was based on an early French name for the region.) A decade later, the park acquired the southern half of Isle au Haut, a small island 15 miles south of Mount Desert Island.

the Father of Acadia
GEORGE DORR

WITHOUT GEORGE DORR, Acadia National Park would not exist as we know it today. His tireless lobbying in Washington, D.C. was responsible for the creation of the park in 1919, and he devoted the rest of his life to preserving and expanding Acadia's holdings.

Dorr first visited Mount Desert Island in 1868 when his wealthy family purchased a summer home in Bar Harbor. As a young man, Dorr attended Oxford University and traveled extensively throughout Europe, exploring the Scottish highlands and hiking the Swiss Alps. When Dorr inherited his family's vast textile fortune at the turn of the century, he could have lived anywhere in the world. His choice: Mount Desert Island, where he could spend his days immersed in outdoor activities. When he wasn't hiking or biking across the island, he was hard at work building new trails and paths for such pursuits. Locals never ceased to marvel at his boundless energy, which included a frigid morning swim in the Atlantic each morning until Christmas.

As his good friend Charles Eliot once put it, "George Dorr is an impulsive, enthusiastic, eager person who works at high tension, neglects his meals, sits up too late at night, and rushes about from one pressing thing to another. But he is very diligent, as well as highly inventive."

In 1944, at the age of 94, George Dorr died an impoverished man. He had spent his entire fortune purchasing additional land for Acadia National Park. Toward the end of his life, shabby clothes replaced once expensive suits, and he could not even afford to buy new books. His estate, once valued at over $10 million, had $2,000 for his funeral only because its trustees had secretly set the money aside, preventing Dorr from giving it all away.

Reflecting on the creation of Acadia National Park, Dorr once noted, "It never will be given up to private ownership again. The men in control will change. The government itself will change. But its possession, by the people, will remain."

Millionaire's Row, after the fire

THE GREAT FIRE OF 1947

BY THE TIME Acadia National Park was established, Bar Harbor was a town in decline. The Cottage Era had started to fade following the introduction of the personal income tax in 1913, and its fate was sealed by the Great Depression. By the late 1940s many of Bar Harbor's once grand mansions had fallen into disrepair.

The next tumultuous chapter in the island's history began on a dry October day in 1947, a year in which a record drought had engulfed the state. That summer and fall, Maine received just 50 percent of its normal rainfall. By mid-October, Mount Desert Island was experiencing the driest conditions ever recorded. On October 17, at the height of the drought, a small fire broke out in the town dump north of Bar Harbor. Firefighters managed to control the blaze, but they were unable to completely put it out. When the fire started to grow, firefighters from across the state were dispatched to prevent a possible catastrophe.

For six days firefighters battled the stubborn blaze. Then, just when the fire was about to be declared out of control, gale force winds descended on Mount Desert Island, whipping up even more flames with 60 mph gusts. It was a nightmare scenario. At 4pm the fire covered 2,000 acres. Eight hours later, over 16,000 acres had burned. "It looked like two gigantic doors had opened and towering columns of roaring flames shot down," recalled one firefighter. Many trees in the fire's path simply exploded as extreme heat pressurized their moist interiors.

Fueled by the howling winds, the fire raced along the northeastern shore of Mount Desert Island and approached Bar Harbor. A lucky shift in wind pushed the fire south, sparing the downtown section, but the fire's destruction blocked all roads leading out of town. To evacuate the trapped citizens, fishermen from nearby towns were dispatched to the Bar Harbor town pier. Over 400 people escaped by boat before bulldozers cleared a path through the rubble north of town. Shortly thereafter, a caravan of 700 cars fled to safety along Route 3 as sparks from the lingering fire shot past their vehicles.

South of Bar Harbor the fire continued to rage, roaring around the eastern edge of the island with no signs of slowing down. As it approached Sand Beach, another lucky shift in wind pushed the fire to the tip of Great Head Peninsula. With winds pounding the inferno, flames leapt nearly a mile over the ocean, forcing nearby sailors to turn away to avoid igniting their sails. But confined to the peninsula, the fire's progress was finally contained.

On October 27, the fire was officially declared under control. But two weeks later, even after rain and snow had fallen, scattered fires continued to smolder below ground. On November 14, the fire was finally declared out. It had burned over 17,000 acres (10,000 in Acadia) and caused five deaths. It had also destroyed nearly $20 million worth of property, including five hotels, 127 homes, and 67 mansions along once-fabled "Millionaires Row."

PRESENT DAY

AS THE SCARS of the fire started to heal, the island took on a new character that defined it for several decades. Although the fire destroyed much of Bar Harbor's gilded era, the island was no longer confronted with its reputation as a faded bastion of wealth. With Acadia National Park acting as its main draw, Mount Desert Island began to attract a new type of visitor: vacationing middle-class families.

To accommodate the new arrivals, dozens of budget hotels and campgrounds sprang up around the park. Bar Harbor reinvented itself as a sleepy tourist town full of fried seafood shacks and nautical trinket stores. But as visitation increased year after year, the town grew increasingly less sleepy and increasingly more upscale. By the end of the century, it had become one of the most popular summer destinations in New England.

Today the economy of Mount Desert Island revolves around tourism. Acadia National Park is tied with L.L. Bean's flagship store in Freeport, Maine, as the state's most visited destination (roughly 3 million visitors annually), and each year over 100 cruise ships drop anchor in Bar Harbor. Although summer is by far the busiest season on the island, more visitors are arriving in the fall, when the crowds are light and the weather is crisp. Not long ago, Labor Day was considered the end of the tourist season. Today, many hotels, shops and restaurants stay open through October to accommodate the leaf-peeping crowd. But by November most business are closed and the island is back in the hands of the locals.

Today year-round residents have a surprisingly wide variety of career options. In addition to fishing and boatbuilding, occupations that have flourished here for hundreds of years, Mount Desert Island has become a hotbed of scientific research. The Jackson Lab, the largest employer in Hancock County, is a world-renowned mammalian research facility with over 1,400 employees. Since it was founded in 1929, over 20 Nobel Prizes have been linked to the lab, which breeds hundreds of strains of genetically pure research mice. (Locals have affectionately nicknamed the lab "the Mouse House.") In addition, the Mount Desert Island Biological Laboratory is at the forefront of genetic research in marine biology.

Bar Harbor's College of the Atlantic (COA) has also had a profound impact on the culture of the island. Founded in 1969, COA offers a single major: human ecology, which explores how humans interact with the environment. Not surprisingly, COA students are a rather crunchy bunch. But their boundless enthusiasm for the natural world finds plenty of productive outlets on Mount Desert Island—from volunteering for Acadia National Park to assisting whale watch researchers at Allied Whale (p.79) In addition to COA's 300 active students, dozens of alumni choose to stay on Mount Desert Island after graduation because they simply can't imagine living anywhere else.

College of the Atlantic

For many year-round locals, the problem these days isn't finding a job, it's finding a house. As wealthy individuals have snatched up summer homes over the past three decades, real-estate prices have skyrocketed. The total value of all private property on Mount Desert Island is now over 4.6 *billion dollars*. A rising tide may lift all boats, but many locals on a tight budget are finding it harder and harder to pay their property taxes. As a result, many people and businesses have moved off the island. Lobstermen may launch their boats from the island's harbors each morning, but many of them live on the mainland and commute.

These days, Mount Desert Island appears to be firmly in the grip of a Second Cottage Era. On summer weekends the Bar Harbor Airport is crowded with dozens of private jets, and private megayachts are becoming a common sight. But this new Cottage Era appears to be distinctly different from the first. These days there's considerable social pressure from Old Money families to downplay wealth (after they climb out of their Gulfstreams, of course). And the shameless social climbing that defined Bar Harbor in the late 1800s has migrated to other, trendier locales. On Mount Desert Island, ostentatious displays are frowned upon, fleece is considered haute couture, and hiking remains the distinguished activity of choice.

For the moment Mount Desert Island continues to fly somewhat under the national radar, commanding nowhere near the same name recognition as Martha's Vineyard or Nantucket, two islands of comparable size yet wide reaching fame. Whether or not Mount Desert Island will continue to remain one of New England's best kept secrets—only time will tell.

ACADIA NATIONAL PARK

As NATIONAL PARKS go, Acadia is posh. Real posh. The wealthy families that flooded the island in the late 1800s may have brought some blue-blooded attitude, but they also brought lots of cash. And when they decided to create Acadia National Park, no expense was spared. Hiking trails were built with exquisite hand-cut stones. The Park Loop Road was designed by America's leading landscape architect. And John D. Rockefeller, Jr. personally commissioned a network of gravel roads through the island's forests exclusively for horse-drawn carriages— *horse-drawn carriages!*

Acadia's scenery is scattered in non-contiguous chunks along the coast of Downeast Maine. The largest and most famous part of the park covers 30,000 acres on Mount Desert Island (roughly 40% of the island). But Acadia also includes 2,400 acres on Schoodic Peninsula (5 miles east on the mainland), 2,700 acres on Isle au Haut (a large island 15 miles to the southwest), and about half a dozen tiny offshore islands.

If you're only here for a weekend, focus your time on Mount Desert Island and the park's most spectacular sights. The Park Loop Road (p.137) is the most famous attraction, but Acadia's 100-mile plus network of hiking trails (p.21) is truly world-class, offering spectacular coastal views. And no visit to Acadia is complete without exploring the popular Rockefeller carriage roads (p.199). Also keep in mind that nearly all of Acadia's popular sights on Mount Desert Island are serviced by the free Island Explorer Shuttle (p.34).

If you're here for a week—or you've already explored Mount Desert Island—Schoodic Peninsula (p.209) and Isle au Haut (p.217) are definitely worth a visit, especially if you're looking to get away from the crowds. (Isle au Haut is as close as to solitude as you'll get in July and August.)

Before you go anywhere, however, purchase a park pass at Hulls Cove Visitor Center (p.138), Thompson Island Visitor Center (p.34), the Bar Harbor Village Green (p.228), Blackwoods or Seawall campgrounds (p.35), or the entrance station near Schooner Head on the Park Loop Road. A seven-day pass costs $20, and an annual pass costs $40. Another option is America The Beautiful Pass ($80), which grants you access to all U.S. national parks and federal lands for one year. Also be sure to pick up a copy of the *Beaver Log*, Acadia's free publication that lists current park openings/closures, ranger programs, tide schedules, sunrise/sunset times, and a wealth of other useful information.

PARK LOOP ROAD

THE PARK LOOP ROAD is Acadia's star attraction. Twisting 27 miles through the spectacular eastern half of Mount Desert Island, it cruises through forests, dips through valleys, skirts the shoreline, and rambles past beautiful lakes and ponds. After passing Acadia's most popular sites—Sand Beach, Thunder Hole, the Jordan Pond House, Bubble Rock—the road climbs to the top of Cadillac Mountain—at 1,530 feet, the island's highest peak.

The Park Loop Road is the main artery of the park, pumping millions of visitors through Acadia each year. But no matter how crowded it gets (and during peak season it can get *very* crowded), the Park Loop Road is always worth it. If you only have one afternoon to spend in the park, spend it on the Park Loop Road.

There are three popular ways to explore the Park Loop Road: drive your own car, pay for a guided bus tour, or take the free Island Explorer Shuttle. All have their pros and cons. Taking your own car offers the most flexibility, but traffic and parking can be a hassle during peak season in July and August. Guided tours (p.231) offer narrated commentary and remove the hassle of driving and parking, but they whisk you through the park on a set schedule with little time to explore interesting sights on your own. The Island Explorer (p.34) offers flexibility (it stops at popular destinations about every 30 minutes) and relaxation (no driving, no parking), but it doesn't follow the Park Loop Road in a continuous loop (it's broken up into two separate routes) and it doesn't go to the top of Cadillac Mountain. Whatever method you choose, plan on spending at least three hours exploring the Park Loop Road. If you do drive your own car, the best place to start is the Hulls Cove Visitor Center (p.138), north of Bar Harbor off Route 3.

The Park Loop Road was the brainchild of John D. Rockefeller, Jr., who realized the enormous potential that a motor road through the park would have. Despite strong opposition from some summer residents, who felt the road would ruin the park, Rockefeller spearheaded construction in 1922. The way Rockefeller saw it, automobiles were inevitable. The park could either thoughtfully plan for their arrival or ignore the issue until it was too late. To ensure that the Park Loop Road blended in peacefully with the natural scenery, Rockefeller commissioned renowned landscape architect Frederick Law Olmsted, Jr., whose father had designed New York's Central Park. Completed in 1953, the Park Loop Road remains one of the most beautiful drives in any national park.

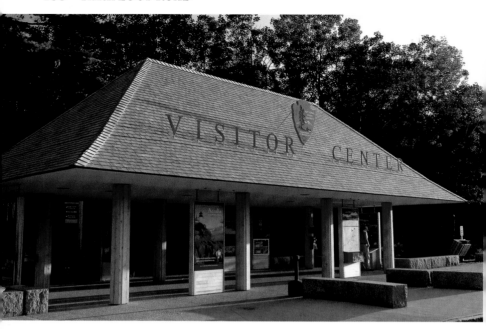

1 Hulls Cove Visitor Center

At the start of the Park Loop Road is Acadia National Park's main visitor center (207-288-3338). There's a large parking area and an Island Explorer shuttle stop. From late-June to mid-October, it's possible to leave your car here and continue by shuttle. A 52-step staircase ascends from the parking area to the visitor center. (People with disabilities can use an alternate parking area reached via a short road at the south end of the main parking area.) Inside you'll find a help desk, free park publications like the *Beaver Log*, a giant relief map of the island, restrooms, and a store overflowing with books, calendars and assorted goodies. A small auditorium also shows a free 15-minute movie about the park. The visitor center is open mid-April through October, 8am-4:30pm (8am to 6pm in July and August). During peak summer months, up to 9,000 people pass through the visitor center each day. It's busiest between 10am and 2pm, so try to arrive earlier or later if you can.

Rules of the Park Loop Road

- The speed limit never exceeds 35 mph, and it is strictly enforced.

- Parking is allowed on the right-hand side of the road between mile 3 and mile 19 (the one-way section of the loop).

2 Frenchman Bay Overlook

The first viewpoint you'll come to on the Park Loop Road overlooks Frenchman Bay, which lies between Mount Desert Island and Schoodic Peninsula to the east. From the overlook you can see several of the Porcupine Islands (p.174), which lie just off Bar Harbor. The closest island to the overlook is Bar Island, which is connected to Bar Harbor twice a day at low tide by a shallow sandbar (p.226). Although the Frenchman Bay Overlook is nice, you'll be treated to much better views of the Porcupine Islands farther down the Park Loop Road.

Frenchman Bay, sans "s"

Grammar nerds take note! The name of the beautiful bay just east of Mount Desert Island is Frenchman Bay, not Frenchman's Bay (with a possessive "s"). Acadia National Park, being a good grammatical citizen, always spells it right. But as you wander outside the park on Mount Desert Island, you'll undoubtedly encounter maps, signs and menus that refer to "Frenchman's Bay."

3 **1947** Fire Overlook

In 1947 Maine suffered its worst drought in decades. After a summer and fall with very little rain, Mount Desert Island experienced the driest conditions ever recorded. Then, in mid-October, a massive fire broke out that burned over 17,000 acres—nearly half the eastern side of Mount Desert Island (p.131).

Before the fire, the island had been dominated by evergreen forests of spruce and fir. These dark, shady forests deterred the growth of sun-loving deciduous tree species, but the 1947 fire dramatically shook up the landscape. At first only blueberry bushes, wildflowers and small ground plants grew in the fire's charred wake. But later a wide range of sun-loving broad-leafed deciduous trees such as birch and poplar took root in the sunny, open spaces created by the fire. This new mixed deciduous forest diversified the landscape, created new habitat for wildlife such as deer and songbirds, and resulted in brilliant fall foliage displays. But as the deciduous trees have flourished, they have created a nursery for shade-loving spruce and fir, which may one day muscle out the colorful deciduous trees and reclaim their lost territory.

From the 1947 Fire Overlook you can still trace the path of the fire, marked by the light green patches of deciduous leaves against the dark green evergreens in the summer. This contrast becomes surreal in the fall, when the deciduous trees' brilliant yellow, orange and red leaves seem to reenact the historic blaze.

4 Sieur de Monts Spring

This peaceful, wooded setting is home to a natural spring that was once used by Indians and early settlers. In many ways, it is the spiritual home of the park. The area around the spring was one of the first pieces of property acquired by George Dorr (p.129), who was one of the driving forces behind the creation of Acadia National Park. Dorr purchased the property in a last-minute deal, snatching it away from real-estate speculators who, aware of Dorr's interest in acquiring land for a park, hoped to buy it first and drive up the price. Dorr later described Sieur de Monts Spring as "one of the foundations on which the future park was built."

Today the spring is covered by an arched dome built by Dorr, who also had "Sweet Waters of Acadia" inscribed on a nearby rock. The inscription was inspired by Dorr's travels in Turkey, where he had seen springs labeled "Sweet Waters of Europe" and "Sweet Waters of Asia." Sieur de Monts Spring was one of Dorr's favorite places, and today Dorr Mountain rises above the spring to the southwest. Due to its wet, wooded location, the area around Sieur de Monts Spring is an excellent spot for bird watching. Over 70 bird species have been identified here.

Next to the parking area is the **Acadia Nature Center**, which offers exhibits about Acadia's native species, and information about efforts to preserve and protect the park's natural resources. There's also a desk where friendly park rangers answer any questions you might have, and ranger talks are sometimes given outside. Just up the hill from the nature center is the small **Abbe Museum** ($3.00 admission), which displays artifacts from local Indian tribes. Among the objects on display are stone tools, weapons, pottery and small flutes carved from animal bones. The museum, open since 1928, displays native artifacts collected by summer resident Robert Abbe. Today this museum is overshadowed by the Abbe's much larger sister museum in downtown Bar Harbor (p.228), but the impressive collection of artifacts here still makes a visit worthwhile. A small gift shop inside also sells baskets and jewelry made by native artists.

Finally, the **Wild Gardens of Acadia**, located adjacent to the parking area, are filled with over 400 species of native flowers, trees, shrubs and other plants. If you're interested in the local flora, it's definitely worth a stroll along the garden's rambling paths. The Wild Gardens of Acadia are open from dawn to dusk.

5 Beaver Dam Pond

This small pond is home to several beavers, whose dam is visible at the far side of the pond. Beavers are most active at dawn and at dusk, so keep your eyes out for ripples in the water if you visit the pond during these times. By 1900 trappers had exterminated beavers from Mount Desert Island, but in 1920 two beaver pairs were successfully reintroduced to the park by George Dorr. The large buildings across the Park Loop Road from the pond belong to the Jackson Lab (p.132)

Sieur de Monts Springs

Beaver Pond

Egg Rock Overlook

Marked by an obvious pull-off on the left side of the road, this overlook provides sweeping views of Frenchman Bay, Egg Rock Lighthouse, and Schoodic Peninsula beyond. Egg Rock was named by early coastal settlers who gathered seabird eggs on its rocky ledges. Egg gathering was later banned when several seabird species, such as eider ducks and herring gulls, nearly went extinct.

In 1875 Egg Rock Lighthouse was built to help ships navigate the rocky entrance to Frenchman Bay. Because Egg Rock is so small, the lighthouse beacon was built on top of the keeper's residence to conserve space. (Most lighthouses place their beacon in a separate tower). For over a century, Egg Rock was manned by lighthouse keepers, who lived year-round on the island and rowed four miles to shore for supplies. The beacon was originally lit by whale oil, which was stored in barrels in the adjacent shack. Whale oil was later replaced by kerosene, which was then replaced by electricity from gas-powered generators. Today the lighthouse is fully automated. Electricity is delivered from Bar Harbor via an underwater cable, and solar panels provide backup energy.

As guardian of Frenchman Bay, Egg Rock has seen some remarkable comings and goings over the years. During World War II a 250-foot German submarine snuck past Egg Rock and deposited two spies at Hancock Point, just north of Mount Desert Island. The spies, carrying $60,000 cash and a bag of diamonds, made their way to New York City before they were captured.

HIGHSEAS

This spectacular brick mansion, perched above the ocean just south of Egg Rock Overlook, was built in 1912 by Princeton professor Rudolf Brunnow. The 32-room mansion was intended as a wedding gift for Brunnow's fiancée, who was then living in Europe. Tragically, his fiancée booked her passage to America on the Titanic, and she perished in the North Atlantic.

In 1924 Highseas was purchased by wealthy New York City divorcée Mrs. Eva Van Cortland Hawkes. The sum: $25,000. Mrs. Hawkes kept a large staff at Highseas that included a butler, two footmen, a downstairs maid, upstairs maid, kitchen maid, personal maid, cook, laundress, cleaning woman, chauffeur and gardener. During World War II, Mrs. Hawkes threw lavish parties at Highseas for the American and British navies that called to port in Bar Harbor. Champagne flowed freely and lobster Newburg was cooked in 30-gallon drums.

When the great fire of 1947 swept through this part of the island, Highseas was spared destruction by a faithful gardener who kept the mansion doused with water. Following Mrs. Hawkes' death, the estate was donated to the Jackson Lab. Today the building is used as a dormitory for high school and college students participating in the Jackson Lab's exclusive Summer Student Program—which counts *three* Nobel Prize winners among its alumni.

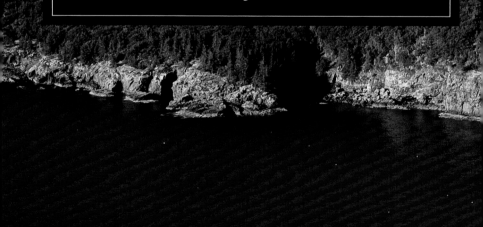

6 Champlain Mountain

Past Egg Rock Overlook, the road descends alongside the sheer eastern flank of Champlain Mountain, which rises nearly 1,000 vertical feet above the Park Loop Road. These cliffs—the steepest on the island—are home to the famous Precipice Trail (p.184), which starts from a small parking area on the right side of the road. In the spring and early summer, the Precipice Trail is often closed to protect nesting peregrine falcons. During this time the park sets up viewing scopes in the parking area from 9am to noon.

Peregrine falcons (p.84) are one of Acadia's most fascinating birds. In the 1960s peregrines faced extinction due to hunting, a reduction in prey, and the effects of the pesticide DDT. The last known nesting pair on Mount Desert Island was seen in 1956, and by 1969 they had completely disappeared from the island.

Following the passage of the Endangered Species Act, conservationists set out to restore peregrine populations in the Eastern U.S. In 1984 peregrine chicks were reintroduced to Acadia National Park as part of a captive breeding program. The chicks were hatched in captivity, then transferred to nesting sites in Acadia when they were 3 to 4 weeks old. Over the next several weeks, trained specialists monitored the chicks and made "food drops" through long tubes, which were designed to prevent the chicks from associating food with humans. Eventually, when their wings were strong enough to fly, the chicks fledged and hunted on their own.

Between 1984 and 1986, over 20 chicks were raised in Acadia. In 1987 captive bred chicks began returning to Acadia as adults, but none produced any young. Then, in 1991, a successful peregrine nesting occurred in Acadia for the first time in 35 years. Over the past two decades, nesting peregrines in Acadia have produced nearly 100 chicks, 60 of which have fledged from the Precipice. Peregrine recovery efforts, like those in Acadia, have been so successful that peregrine falcons have been removed from the endangered species list.

7 Schooner Head

Just before the park entrance station, a short spur road heads left to an overlook with dramatic views of Schooner Head and Egg Rock Lighthouse. Schooner Head is named for several white markings that resemble the sails of a ship when viewed from sea. During the American Revolutionary War, a British warship supposedly fired upon Schooner Head during a snow squall, mistaking the white markings for an American ship. A short path descends from the Schooner Head parking area to some rocky cliffs below.

The giant, modern house perched on top of Schooner Head is owned by Dan Burt, a wealthy attorney-turned-poet. Burt once told a local newspaper that he had traveled all over the world, but "I've never seen a piece of land or area more beautiful than Mount Desert."

Peregrine Falcon Chicks

🔟 Thunder Hole

Thunder Hole is a narrow rock crevice that booms like thunder when the waves hit it just right. The trick is to visit at just the right time (about two hours before high tide) and in just the right seas (about three to six feet). With luck and timing, you might hear the famous booming sound. So why does Thunder Hole thunder? At the end of the crevice is a small cave. When waves rush into the cave, they trap and compress the air inside. As pressure builds inside the cave, the air explodes outward in a burst of spray, producing a booming, thundering sound.

But don't get your hopes up. Although Thunder Hole is one of Acadia's most famous sights, many visitors walk away disappointed. Expecting dramatic booms, all they hear are gurgles and sloshes. But "Sloshing Hole" or "Hole That Thunders Only Occasionally" is no name for a star attraction.

That said, when stormy seas descend upon the coast of Maine, Thunder Hole is one of the most spectacular sights on the island. Unlike much of Mount Desert Island, which is sheltered by small offshore islands, Thunder Hole is almost fully exposed to the open ocean. In high seas, waves crash here with a fury that has to be seen to be believed. But if you do visit during a storm, please use caution and don't wander out onto the nearby rocks. The photos on these pages were taken on August 23, 2009, when the remnants of Hurricane Bill kicked up 15-20 foot seas in the Gulf of Maine. As I was taking these photos, a large wave swept a father and his 7-year-old daughter off the rocks just south of Thunder Hole and into the 55-degree water. Although the Coast Guard rescued the father, the little girl drowned.

Monument Cove

11 Monument Cove

Most people drive past Monument Cove without even realizing it's there. But this tiny cove, sheltered by tall pine trees on either side, is a testament to the power of erosion. The "monument" of the cove is the obelisk-like spire at the north end. Over thousands of years, erosion widened natural cracks in the rocks surrounding the cove. As rock chunks fell away, the monument was left behind. The fallen chunks were then tumbled by the waves, eroding to form rounded, pumpkin-sized boulders. Like Sand Beach, Monument Cove is partially sheltered from waves and currents. But here, where the cove is much more exposed to the ocean, waves and currents are powerful enough to wash away any sand or small cobblestones that might form, leaving only heavy boulders behind.

12 Otter Cliffs

These vertical cliffs rise 110 feet above the ocean, making them irresistible to rock climbers who scamper up the sheer walls nearly every day in the summer and fall. In fact, Otter Cliffs is one of the only places on the eastern seaboard where you can rock climb directly above the ocean. (If you're interested in taking rock climbing lessons, there are two good outfitters in Bar Harbor, p.27) Despite Otter Cliff's name, there are no sea otters here. In fact, there are no sea otters on the entire East Coast. Otter Cliffs and Otter Point—as well as Otter Cove and Otter Creek—were probably named after river otters (which are found in Acadia) or the now-extinct sea mink, which was sometimes mistaken for an otter.

13 Otter Point

About half a mile past Otter Cliffs, the parking area for Otter Point appears on your right. From the parking area a short path crosses the road and heads down to the rocky shore at Otter Point, which at low tide is one of the best places in the park to explore tidepools. Head towards the southwestern tip of Otter Point to find the largest and most impressive tidepools. Look close and you can probably find barnacles, dog whelks, sea stars and other creatures of the intertidal zone (p.66).

14 Fabbri Picnic Area

This small picnic area is a good place to stop if you brought a picnic lunch. Across from the picnic area is a memorial that commemorates a strategically important naval radio station that operated here during World War I. The station received important information from the European front, but in 1932 it was relocated to Schoodic Peninsula to make way for the Park Loop Road.

Otter Cliffs

Otter Cliffs

Little Hunters Beach

This unmarked cobblestone beach, reached by a small wooden staircase on the left side of the road, is a geologist's delight. The cobblestones here formed from rocks in Acadia's "Shatter Zone." Roughly 370 million years ago, a large plume of magma rose up under Mount Desert Island's previously formed bedrock and cooled into granite. But when the scorching hot magma came into contact with the cool bedrock above, the bedrock shattered into pieces. Some of those pieces fell into the magma, and when the magma cooled into granite the pieces were suspended in the granite like plums in plum pudding. These "plum pudding" rocks make up the Shatter Zone. At Little Hunters Beach you can often see chunks of the older, mostly darker bedrock (the "plums") in the granite cobblestones. The rusty coloration found on some rocks is due to iron oxide.

15 Wildwood Stables

Wildwood Stables offers horse-drawn buckboard rides ranging from one to two hours on Acadia's famous Carriage Roads. Three trips are available: Day Mountain, which offers sweeping views of the coast; Cobblestone Bridge, a pleasant ride through the forest to an exquisite stone bridge; and the Jordan Pond House, where tea and popovers are served on the lawn. Private carriage rides are also available. (Open mid-June to mid-Oct, 207-276-3622, www.acadia.net/wildwood)

16 Jordan Pond Gatehouse

In 1932 John D. Rockefeller, Jr. had this gatehouse built as a checkpoint to keep automobiles off the Carriage Roads. (Today it serves as a residence for lucky park personnel.) Rockefeller felt the architecture in many national parks was random and haphazard, and he was determined to make Acadia's buildings better. In 1929 he sent architect Grosvenor Atterbury on a tour of national parks to study their architectural successes and faults. Atterbury returned with several guidelines for successful national park architecture, most importantly: (1) buildings should not compete with the local scenery, and (2) if no local style of architecture exists for reference, a suitable foreign style should be chosen. Because no local style existed in Acadia, Atterbury designed the Jordan Pond Gatehouse based on a French Romanesque design. The gatehouse also features whimsical details such as birdhouses in the garage gables and shutters with the letter "A" for Atterbury.

Wildwood Stables

☑ 17 Jordan Pond House

The Jordan Pond House is one of the highlights of Acadia. For over a century, visitors have come here to feast on the food and the scenery. Lunch and dinner are served, but the main attraction is the house specialty: popovers, large, steamy pastries that are part muffin, part balloon. Oven-fresh popovers would be mouth-watering in any part of the world. But here in front of Jordan Pond, they are truly divine. The menu also includes stews, chowders, salads and entrees like baked scallops and lobster quiche ($10–17). The restaurant is open mid-May to mid-October, and reservations are available: 207-276-3316. In the summer the last Island Explorer shuttle leaves Jordan Pond at 8:45 pm.

The original Jordan Pond House opened its doors in 1896. Back then, it was little more than a rambling, birchbark farmhouse, and visitors would arrive on foot via hiking trails from Seal Harbor. Later John D. Rockefeller, Jr. bought the property and donated it to the park. Sadly, a fire destroyed the original Jordan Pond House in 1979. The modern building was built in 1982.

At 150 feet, Jordan Pond is the deepest body of freshwater on the island. At the north end of Jordan Pond lie the Bubbles, two glacially rounded mountains that appear to be symmetrical. In fact, this view is an optical illusion. North Bubble, on the left, is actually 100 feet taller than South Bubble. But because it's set 2,000 feet back, it appears to be the same height. You can walk to the base of the Bubbles along the Jordan Pond Trail, a moderate 3.2-mile hike that loops around the perimeter of Jordan Pond.

Jordan Pond House, early 1900s

Jordan Pond from South Bubble

18 Bubble Rock

As the Park Loop Road rises above the eastern shore of Jordan Pond, it heads between Pemetic Mountain (on your right) and the Bubbles (on your left). Keep your eyes out for rock climbers on the cliffs of South Bubble, then shift your gaze upward for a glimpse of Bubble Rock. Perched precariously on a high ledge, this 14-ton boulder was deposited by a melting glacier roughly 15,000 years ago. Geologists refer to such rocks as *glacial erratics*, and Bubble Rock is one of the most famous glacial erratics in the world.

As massive glaciers advanced over Maine during the last glaciation, loose rocks and boulders were picked up and carried along by the moving ice. Bubble Rock was one of those boulders, and geologists believe it was picked up somewhere near Lucerne Lake, roughly 20 miles to the northwest. By the time Bubble Rock was carried over the top of South Bubble, global temperatures warmed and the glacier stopped advancing. As the glacier slowly melted, Bubble Rock settled on top of South Bubble in the precarious position you see today.

Although Bubble Rock looks like it could topple over at any moment, it's actually quite secure. You can see for yourself via the short Bubble Rock Trail, a moderate, 0.7 mile round-trip trail that starts from the Bubble Rock parking area. A close examination of Bubble Rock reveals black and white crystals that are distinct from the pinkish crystals found in South Bubble's bedrock. Even if you're not interested in geology, a walk to the top of South Bubble is worth it for the stunning views of Jordan Pond not far from Bubble Rock.

19 Bubble Pond

Nestled between Cadillac and Pemetic Mountains, Bubble Pond rests in a graceful, U-shaped valley that's a tell-tale sign of a glacially carved landscape. A carriage road curves around the western shore (great for a quick stroll), but swimming here is prohibited because the pond is a public water supply. The stone bridge next to the pond is unique in the carriage road system because it's the only bridge made entirely of stone. Most carriage road bridges are made of reinforced concrete covered with cut stone.

20 Eagle Lake Overlook

This small overlook offers sweeping views of Eagle Lake, the second largest lake on Mount Desert Island after Long Pond. In the late 1800s, before the Park Loop Road existed, the steamship *Wauwinnet* ferried tourists across Eagle Lake to the base of Cadillac Mountain. From there the tourists would board a small cog railroad that took them to the top of Cadillac. The venture was not profitable, however, and the *Wauwinnet* was sunk in Eagle Lake, where it rests today.

Jordan Pond from South Bubble

18 Bubble Rock

As the Park Loop Road rises above the eastern shore of Jordan Pond, it heads between Pemetic Mountain (on your right) and the Bubbles (on your left). Keep your eyes out for rock climbers on the cliffs of South Bubble, then shift your gaze upward for a glimpse of Bubble Rock. Perched precariously on a high ledge, this 14-ton boulder was deposited by a melting glacier roughly 15,000 years ago. Geologists refer to such rocks as *glacial erratics*, and Bubble Rock is one of the most famous glacial erratics in the world.

As massive glaciers advanced over Maine during the last glaciation, loose rocks and boulders were picked up and carried along by the moving ice. Bubble Rock was one of those boulders, and geologists believe it was picked up somewhere near Lucerne Lake, roughly 20 miles to the northwest. By the time Bubble Rock was carried over the top of South Bubble, global temperatures warmed and the glacier stopped advancing. As the glacier slowly melted, Bubble Rock settled on top of South Bubble in the precarious position you see today.

Although Bubble Rock looks like it could topple over at any moment, it's actually quite secure. You can see for yourself via the short Bubble Rock Trail, a moderate, 0.7 mile round-trip trail that starts from the Bubble Rock parking area. A close examination of Bubble Rock reveals black and white crystals that are distinct from the pinkish crystals found in South Bubble's bedrock. Even if you're not interested in geology, a walk to the top of South Bubble is worth it for the stunning views of Jordan Pond not far from Bubble Rock.

19 Bubble Pond

Nestled between Cadillac and Pemetic Mountains, Bubble Pond rests in a graceful, U-shaped valley that's a tell-tale sign of a glacially carved landscape. A carriage road curves around the western shore (great for a quick stroll), but swimming here is prohibited because the pond is a public water supply. The stone bridge next to the pond is unique in the carriage road system because it's the only bridge made entirely of stone. Most carriage road bridges are made of reinforced concrete covered with cut stone.

20 Eagle Lake Overlook

This small overlook offers sweeping views of Eagle Lake, the second largest lake on Mount Desert Island after Long Pond. In the late 1800s, before the Park Loop Road existed, the steamship *Wauwinnet* ferried tourists across Eagle Lake to the base of Cadillac Mountain. From there the tourists would board a small cog railroad that took them to the top of Cadillac. The venture was not profitable, however, and the *Wauwinnet* was sunk in Eagle Lake, where it rests today.

Porcupine Islands

As you drive along the Park Loop Road up Cadillac Mountain, you'll be treated to sweeping northeastern views of Bar Harbor, Frenchman Bay, and the Porcupine Islands. During the French and Indian War, French gunboats hid behind the Porcupine Islands to ambush British vessels, which is probably how Frenchman Bay got its name. Even after the war, the islands continued to make fabulous hiding places. One of the islands, Rum Key, got its name during Prohibition when rum runners smuggled liquor into Frenchman Bay from Canada. Today four of the Porcupine Islands are owned by Acadia National Park. Burnt Island, which is privately owned, belongs to the town of Gouldsboro across Frenchman Bay.

Blue Hill Overlook

The best place to watch sunset on Cadillac Mountain is the
Blue Hill Overlook. From the parking area, almost everyone
follows the crowds to the open area to the right, but the best
views are actually to the left! Follow the sidewalk to some small
steps, then continue over the granite. You'll soon come to an
even higher area with stunning views of Eagle Lake and Blue
Hill, plus dramatic views of the Cranberry Isles to the south.

21 Cadillac Mountain

Saving the best for last, the Park Loop Road heads up a 3.5-mile spur road to the top of Cadillac Mountain. At 1,530 feet, Cadillac is the highest mountain on the island and the highest point on the Atlantic north of Rio de Janeiro. From roughly October 7 to March 7, Cadillac Mountain is the first place in the United States to see the sunrise.

The road to the summit is filled with hairpin turns and spectacular views of the island. A pullout on the right offers western views of Eagle Lake, Sargent Mountain, and the back side of the Bubbles. Continuing on you'll twist around to eastern views of Bar Harbor, the Porcupine Islands, and Frenchman Bay. Then, after a long, straight ascent along the western side of Cadillac, the road wraps around a hairpin turn with a small pullout, which offers great views of the island's southern shore and the smaller islands beyond. Just past the turn is the Blue Hill Overlook, the most popular sunset spot on Mount Desert Island. (Arrive well before sunset during peak season to snag a space in the parking area)

At Cadillac's summit you'll find a large parking area, restrooms and a small store selling gifts and snacks. The 0.3-mile Summit Trail loops around the eastern edge of Cadillac, offering sweeping views of the coast. As you walk around Cadillac, take a moment to imagine the landscape 20,000 years ago when the entire region was covered entirely by ice. At its peak, the glacier that covered much of North America was over a mile thick here, burying the top of Cadillac under several thousand feet of ice and stretching over 200 miles into the Gulf of Maine.

If the crowds on the Summit Trail are crazy—as they often are in the summer—you can probably find solace at Cadillac's *true* peak, reached via a short trail/access road adjacent to the gift shop. Keep your eyes out for the metal USGS marker embedded in the rock and tremendous views of the southern shores of Mount Desert Island and the Cranberry Isles beyond.

Contrary to popular belief, Cadillac's summit does not lie above treeline. But conditions here are so harrowing that, on much of Cadillac's peak, only small, rugged plants survive. Plants living here must cope with strong winds, freezing temperatures, and rapid erosion from run-off. The constant erosion and sparse vegetation lead to poor soil development, which often prevents larger plants, like trees, from taking root. The landscape here is fragile, so watch where you step. Each year millions of visitors explore Cadillac's summit, and all those footsteps add up. The park recommends sticking to Cadillac's half-mile loop trail to preserve the sparse vegetation.

In the late 1800s a small cog railroad chugged up the side of Cadillac (then called Green Mountain). The half-hour ride cost $2.50 and brought visitors to the summit where they could spend the night in the 50-room Summit Hotel. The railroad was short-lived, however, going bankrupt after only a decade. The hotel was torn down in 1896.

Sunrise, Cadillac Mountain

◁ BEEHIVE TRAIL ᐅ

SUMMARY   Short, steep and sweet, the Beehive Trail is one of the most popular trails in Acadia. Rising to the top of a beehive-shaped dome that towers above the Park Loop Road, the trail provides unbeatable views of Sand Beach and Great Head Peninsula. Although the Beehive Trail is one of the shorter trails in Acadia, it's not for the faint of heart. A few steep sections require climbing iron rungs, and several precipitous drop-offs won't sit well with anyone with a fear of heights. If you are afraid of heights, the route up the steep southern face of the Beehive Trail is probably not for you, but you can still enjoy the views from the top via the Bowl Trail, which wraps around the backside of the Beehive. No matter what your approach, be sure to check out the Bowl. This small mountain pond, nestled in the granite behind the Beehive, is a perfect place to soak your feet or jump in for a refreshing swim.

TRAILHEAD   The Bowl Trail starts across the Park Loop Road from the Sand Beach parking area. Follow the Bowl Trail 0.2 miles to its intersection with the Beehive Trail, which veers off to the right.

TRAIL INFO

RATING: Strenuous, Ladder

DISTANCE: 1.6 miles, round-trip

HIKING TIME: 1–2 hours

ELEVATION CHANGE: 520 ft.

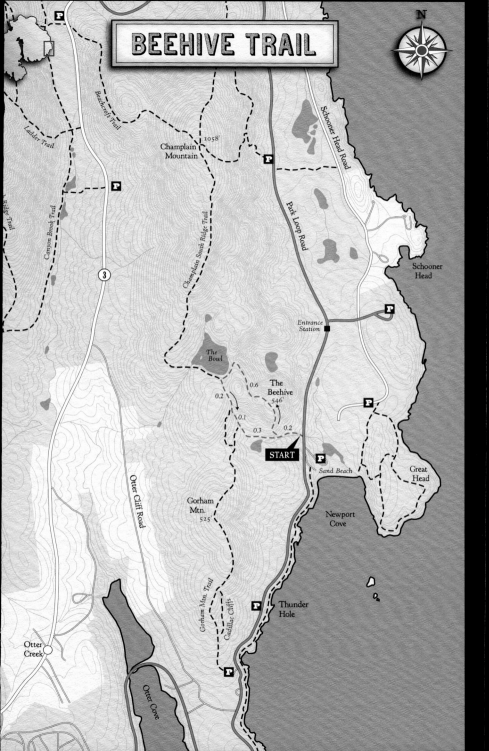

❧ THE PRECIPICE ❧

SUMMARY Rising nearly 1,000 feet up the sheer east face of Champlain Mountain, the Precipice might be the most challenging trail in the park. It's certainly the most famous. A jungle gym of iron rungs guides hikers up this sheer cliff, which offers thrilling ascents and tremendous views of Frenchman Bay. Despite the hype, it takes more mental strength than physical strength to conquer the Precipice. Other than some exposed, 100-foot plus drop-offs and a few steep sections that require ladder-style climbing, the Precipice is no worse than many other challenging, yet less-heralded hikes in Acadia. But if you do have a fear of heights—or if the Precipice is closed due to nesting peregrine falcons—you can still reach the top of Champlain via the 1.2-mile Beachcroft Path, which starts off Route 3. From the summit of Champlain, follow the North Ridge Trail and Orange and Black Path back to return to the Precipice parking area.

TRAILHEAD The Precipice Trail starts from the Precipice parking area off the Park Loop Road, two miles south of Sieur de Monts entrance off Route 3.

TRAIL INFO

RATING: Strenuous, Ladder   **HIKING TIME:** 2–3 hours

DISTANCE: 2.5 miles, round-trip   **ELEVATION CHANGE:** 978 ft.

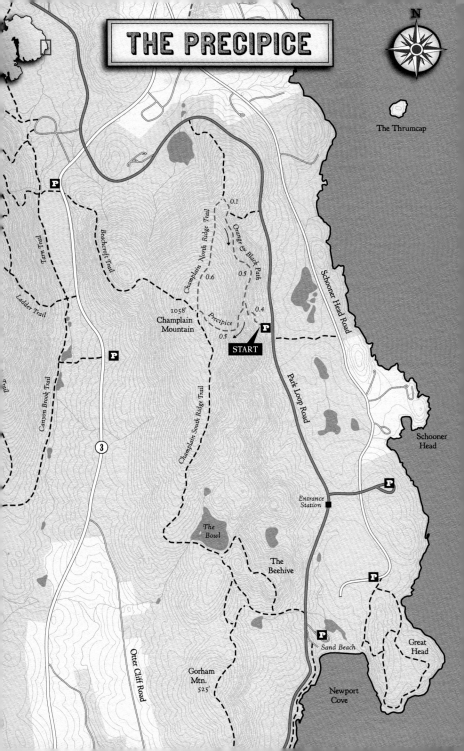

THE PRECIPICE

N

The Thrumcap

P

Tarn Trail

Beachcroft Trail

Ladder Trail

0.1

Orange & Black Path

Champlain North Ridge Trail

0.6

0.5

0.5

0.4

1058'
Champlain
Mountain

Precipice

0.5

P

START

Schooner Head Road

P

Canyon Brook Trail

P

Champlain South Ridge Trail

Park Loop Road

Schooner
Head

3

P

Entrance
Station

The
Bowl

The
Beehive

P

P

Sand Beach

Great
Head

Otter Cliff Road

Gorham
Mtn.
525'

Newport
Cove

✺ GORHAM MOUNTAIN ✺

SUMMARY Gorham Mountain offers the best views of any moderate hike in the park. Great for families with young children, the trail rises to the summit of Gorham Mountain, providing dramatic views of Otter Cliffs, Sand Beach and the gorgeous stretch of shoreline along Ocean Drive. Cadillac Cliffs, a short spur trail that branches off from the main trail, passes by an ancient sea cave that sat at sea level several thousand years ago (at the time, in the wake of the glaciers, the land was compressed and sea levels were much higher). As you climb towards the summit, be sure to turn around and enjoy the dramatic views to the south—they're better than the views from the summit! After reaching the summit, follow the trail north to the Sand Beach parking area. From the parking area stroll back to the Gorham Mountain trailhead along the easy Ocean Path.

TRAILHEAD The Gorham Mountain Trail starts from the Gorham Mountain parking area, located on the right side of the Park Loop Road about half a mile past Thunder Hole.

◆ TRAIL INFO ◆

RATING: Moderate

DISTANCE: 3.2 miles, round-trip

HIKING TIME: 1–2 hours

ELEVATION CHANGE: 525 ft.

⤙ CADILLAC MOUNTAIN ⤚

SUMMARY At 1,530 feet Cadillac Mountain is the island's highest peak, and as such it proves irresistible to many hikers. The best route up Cadillac is the North Ridge Trail, which offers the island's best views of Bar Harbor and the Porcupine Islands. Upon reaching the summit you'll be treated to sweeping, 360-degree views of Mount Desert Island. And though you'll be sharing those views with everyone who arrived by car, rest assured that your endorphin-soaked brain will be enjoying them more! From the summit parking area, follow the dirt path next to the giftshop to the island's true peak (look for the USGS marker embedded in the bedrock) and continue down Cadillac's South Ridge Trail, which offers dramatic views of the island's southern shore. The trail ends at Blackwoods Campground, where you can catch the Island Explorer shuttle back to downtown Bar Harbor.

TRAILHEAD The Cadillac North Ridge trailhead is located along the Park Loop Road, 1/3 of a mile past the Y-intersection where the Park Loop Road becomes one-way. There's a small pull-out across from the trailhead. The Island Explorer "Loop Road" route stops at the Cadillac North Ridge trailhead.

TRAIL INFO

RATING: Strenuous   **HIKING TIME:** 3–4 hours

DISTANCE: 5.7 miles, round-trip   **ELEVATION CHANGE:** 1,463 ft.

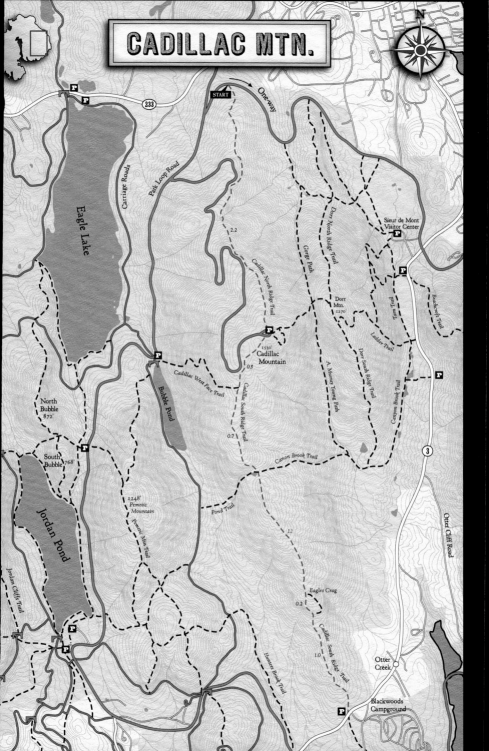

⊰ PENOBSCOT MOUNTAIN ⊱

SUMMARY   Penobscot Mountain is my favorite hike in the Jordan Pond area. The trail to the summit is classic Acadia, climbing up a bare granite ridge with spectacular views of the Gulf of Maine. The trail starts near the Jordan Pond House and rises quickly through dense forest. After scrambling over a few iron rungs, you'll burst onto the vista-soaked granite ridge of Penobscot Mountain. Hiking above treeline, you can see the Cranberry Isles to the south and, if it's a clear day, Great Duck Island and Little Duck Island beyond. After passing over the summit, the trail dips back into the forest and descends rapidly to Jordan Pond along the Deer Brook Trail, which passes under a magnificent carriage road bridge. Once at the northern tip of Jordan Pond, you can follow the Jordan Pond Shore Trail back to the Jordan Pond House. Tip: fresh popovers at the Jordan Pond House are even more delicious after a hike up Penobscot Mountain.

TRAILHEAD   The Penobscot Mountain Trailhead is located behind the Jordan Pond House. Follow the trail into the woods and look for a carved signpost.

TRAIL INFO

RATING: Strenuous

DISTANCE: 3.7 miles, round-trip

HIKING TIME: 2–3 hours

ELEVATION CHANGE: 973 ft.

⚜ SARGENT MOUNTAIN ⚜

SUMMARY   At 1,373 feet Sargent Mountain is Acadia's second highest peak, just 157 feet shy of Cadillac Mountain. Like Cadillac, Sargent has sweeping 360-degree views rolling down from a bare granite summit. Unlike Cadillac, it's not swarming with tourists. In fact, because Sargent Mountain is one of Acadia's most remote and challenging hikes, there's a good chance you'll have the views all to yourself. There are several possible approaches, but my favorite heads up and over Parkman Mountain. From there head up the western face of Sargent Mountain along the Grandgent Trail. As you climb the steep Grandgent Trail, be sure to rest and take in the terrific views of Somesville and Somes Sound to the west. After reaching the summit, head down Sargent's gorgeous southern ridge to the Hadlock Brook Trail, which passes by gurgling streams, shimmering cascades, and one of the Carriage Roads' most spectacular stone bridges.

TRAILHEAD   Head to the small parking area just north of Upper Hadlock Pond, next to the Norumbega Mountain trailhead. The Hadlock Brook Trail starts across the street from the parking area.

TRAIL INFO

RATING: Strenuous

DISTANCE: 4.6 miles, round-trip

HIKING TIME: 4–5 Hours

ELEVATION CHANGE: 1,152 ft.

ACADIA MOUNTAIN

SUMMARY   Acadia Mountain is my favorite trail on the western side of Mount Desert Island. Perched high above Somes Sound, it offers spectacular views of the East Coast's only fjord and the beautiful islands scattered along Mount Desert Island's southern shore. After passing through a shady spruce-fir forest and scrambling over a large granite ledge, the trail climbs to the top of Acadia Mountain. The view from the peak is nice, but an even better view awaits a short distance farther. From there the trail drops roughly 600 feet in half a mile. Near the base of the mountain is a small trail that leads to Man 'o War Brook Waterfall, a small cascade where ships would replenish their water supply in the 18th and 19th century. (The water in Somes Sound is so deep that ships could simply pull up alongside the cascade and fill up their barrels.) From Man 'o War Brook follow the dirt access road back to the trailhead. Tip: after hiking Acadia Mountain, follow the trail from the parking area down to Echo Lake for a refreshing swim!

TRAILHEAD   The trail starts across the street from the Acadia Mountain parking area on Route 102, about two miles north of Southwest Harbor.

TRAIL INFO

RATING: Strenuous

DISTANCE: 2.6-miles, round-trip

HIKING TIME: 2 hours

ELEVATION CHANGE: 581 ft.

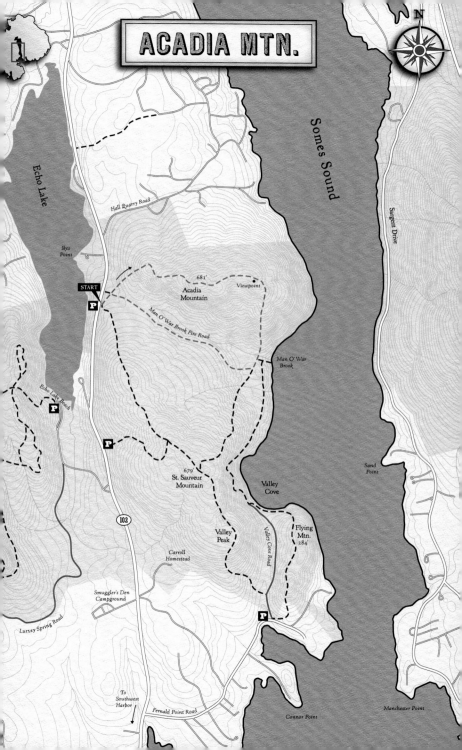

✇ **BEECH MOUNTAIN** ✇

SUMMARY   This peaceful hike, far removed from the crowds on the eastern side of the island, reveals some of the island's most overlooked and underrated scenery. From the Beech Mountain parking area, follow the Valley Trail through a lush spruce-fir forest, then climb a series of exquisite granite steps up the Beech Mountain South Ridge Trail. After a long ascent you'll reach Beech Mountain's peak. From the top you'll enjoy terrific views of the southern shore of western Mount Desert Island. The fire tower on top of Beech Mountain was last used in 1976—today most fire patrols are done by small planes. The tower is closed to the public except on special weekends in the fall (check local papers for details). From the summit follow the western branch of the Beech Mountain Trail back to the parking area. Along the way you'll be treated to gorgeous views of Long Pond.

TRAILHEAD   Follow Route 102 south of Somesville, then turn right onto Pretty Marsh Road. Turn left onto Beech Hill Road, which dead ends at the Beech Mountain parking area. The Valley Trail starts at the south end of the parking area.

◄ TRAIL INFO ►

RATING: Moderate   **HIKING TIME:** 2 hours

DISTANCE: 2.9 miles, round-trip   **ELEVATION CHANGE:** 589 ft.

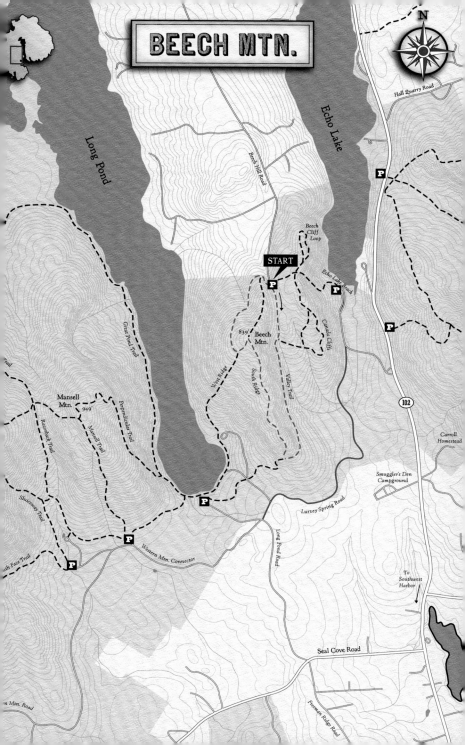

Duck Brook Bridge

CARRIAGE ROADS

ACADIA'S CARRIAGE ROADS are like a fairy tale come to life. Originally constructed on the private estate of John D. Rockefeller, Jr., they were later donated to the park for the enjoyment of the public. Today over 57 miles of gravel roads twist through Acadia, revealing the island's lush interior—a land of leafy forests, sparkling streams, and stunning lakes. Sprinkled along the carriage roads are 17 exquisite stone bridges, hand-crafted by stonemasons out of native rock. When the bridges first opened, they regularly saw the comings and goings of horse-drawn carriages. But today bicycles are the most popular form of transportation along the carriage roads, and many people consider a pedal-powered romp on the carriage roads to be one of the highlights of Acadia National Park.

The carriage roads form a network of car-free roads on the eastern half of Mount Desert Island, extending from Paradise Hill (near downtown Bar Harbor) south to the Rockefeller family estate in Seal Harbor. There is no official start or end to the carriage roads. There are, however, six popular parking areas next to the carriage roads where most people begin their journey. From there you can choose your own adventure. Although the intricate network of roads can be confusing at first, numbered signposts at every intersection make it hard to get lost when you have a good map (p.204–207). Bicycles can be rented in Bar Harbor (p.232), or you can head to Wildwood Stables near Seal Harbor for a genuine horse-drawn carriage ride (p.164). Of course, walking the carriage roads is also an option. (Note: Twelve miles of carriage roads in Seal Harbor are open only to hikers and horseback riders—no bicycles are allowed there. Keep your eyes out for the "No Bicycle" signs posted at intersections.)

The fascinating history of the carriage roads traces its roots to the year 1837, when a wooden bridge first connected Mount Desert Island to the mainland. Before the bridge, Mount Desert Island was only accessible by sea. After the bridge, visitors could arrive by land. For decades this minor improvement produced relatively little change in island life because ships remained the primary mode of transportation. But with the dawn of the automobile age in the late 1800s, the tiny bridge became a vital link between Mount Desert Island and the modern world—a fact that did not sit well with the summer residents who came to Mount Desert Island specifically to *escape* the modern world.

By the time Henry Ford introduced his Model T to the masses in 1908, cars were already banned on Mount Desert Island. The ban served two purposes: it allowed rich summer visitors to take refuge from the sputtering, soot-spewing automobiles that were flourishing in big cities, and it allowed year-round residents to limit the pretentious lifestyles of the rich. All that changed with the introduction of the Model T. As moderately priced cars flooded the nation, local islanders were determined not to be left out of the fun. On a more practical level, cars offered a cheap, efficient method of transport for local businesses. In 1909 a group of locals attempted to repeal the ban on cars, but their efforts were blocked by a group of wealthy summer residents who lobbied hard to keep the ban in place. The locals, vowing revenge, promised to revisit the matter as soon as possible.

Two years later, a temporary compromise was reached limiting cars to the town of Bar Harbor. But when a local man died because a horse-drawn carriage could not reach the hospital in time, the automobile ban was widely denounced. By 1915 cars were allowed in every town on Mount Desert Island.

Among the summer residents most alarmed at this turn of events was John D. Rockefeller, Jr. A recent arrival to Mount Desert Island, Rockefeller had purchased a home in Seal Harbor as a summer refuge from New York City. At a time when most wealthy Manhattan businessmen commuted to work in shiny new cars, Rockefeller drove himself to work in a horse-drawn carriage—a habit that drew considerable attention and spoke volumes about his poor fit among the office buildings of New York. Since birth Rockefeller had been groomed to take over his family's vast oil business. But Rockefeller and Standard Oil were hardly a match made in heaven. Happiest outdoors, Rockefeller coped with the stress of Manhattan office life by chopping wood after work. After a few years at the helm at Standard Oil, he quit the family business, devoted himself to a life of philanthropy, and purchased his 150-acre Seal Harbor estate.

When Rockefeller arrived in Seal Harbor in 1910, the Great Automobile War—as it was later called—was just beginning. Perhaps sensing the inevitable, Rockefeller began building a series of gravel roads on his sprawling Seal Harbor property where he could enjoy the simple pleasures of a horse-drawn carriage ride. As his network of roads grew, he decided to connect them in a continuous loop. To do so, however, required passing through land owned by the Hancock County Trustees of Public Reservations (the predecessor of Acadia National Park). Rockefeller tried to buy the land in question, but his offer was refused. He was allowed, however, to build roads through the land with the knowledge that they might one day be shut down.

Rockefeller accepted this risk, and over the next decade he continued to expand his network of roads through the park. Things went well until one planned road in Northeast Harbor drew heat from local conservationists who felt it would be a blight on the natural landscape. Northeast Harbor summer resident George Wharton Pepper fired off a letter to Rockefeller. "In my judgement," he wrote, "it would be a serious mistake to extend your well conceived system of roads into

JOHN D. ROCKEFELLER, JR.

Without John D. Rockefeller, Jr.'s deep pockets and even deeper sense of philanthropy, many of Acadia's most popular attractions would not exist. He is the park's most famous benefactor, and he embodied the public-minded spirit that defines Acadia.

Rockefeller was born in 1874, the sole male heir to the vast Standard Oil fortune. Influenced by his family's pious values, he was a strict non-drinker and a deeply religious man. He was also a lover of nature, spending as much time as possible outdoors. Although he went to work for Standard Oil after graduating from Brown University, Rockefeller quickly realized that the family business was not for him. In 1910, at the age of 36, he retired from the working world and devoted himself to a life of philanthropy.

Rockefeller first visited Mount Desert Island in college, but it wasn't until he returned in 1908 with his wife, Abbey, that he fell in love with the island. Two years later, Rockefeller bought a spectacular hilltop estate in Seal Harbor, and soon he was approached by local philanthropist George Dorr, who was soliciting funds to preserve land on the island. After hearing Dorr's vision of a national park on Mount Desert Island, Rockefeller enthusiastically opened his wallet.

In the decades to come, Rockefeller would become Acadia's greatest benefactor, donating roughly one-third of the land in the park. Before Rockefeller came along, the park consisted mostly of mountaintops. Rockefeller bought the land in between the mountaintops and donated it to the park. He also spearheaded and financed both the Park Loop Road and the carriage roads—two projects that drew strong opposition at the time. Some conservationists felt the roads would ruin the wild nature of the park, but Rockefeller disagreed. A firm believer that nature could make people "happier, richer, better," Rockefeller argued that roads and paths were necessary to make nature more accessible to the public. Today, few would disagree that Rockefeller's contributions have made the park a better place for all.

How Rich was Rockefeller?

In 1913, shortly before the breakup of Standard Oil, the Rockefeller family fortune was estimated at $900 million—about $20 billion today adjusted for inflation. But when viewed as a percentage of the 1913 Gross National Product, which provides a better measure of the economic clout the Rockefellers wielded at the time, their fortune would have been worth roughly $320 billion today—over six times the net worth of Bill Gates.

this area." Rockefeller reluctantly agreed, and he halted construction of the road in question. But by this point many people were using and enjoying the roads that were already built. In fact, many locals openly supported Rockefeller's plans. A group of locals circulated a petition urging Rockefeller to continue construction, and the *Bar Harbor Times* published an op-ed in full support of the carriage roads. But despite the outpouring of support, the ever-cautious Rockefeller stayed out of the fray and did not resume construction of the road in question.

The sudden controversy was particularly worrisome to George Dorr, the savvy superintendant of the park. Dorr knew that Rockefeller's deep pockets were essential to acquire additional land for the park, and he did not want to alienate the park's wealthiest benefactor. Recognizing Rockefeller's obvious enthusiasm for road building, Dorr suggested that Rockefeller help build an "access" road next to Jordan Pond. Rockefeller jumped at the idea, and by 1921 the "access" road had expanded to include a series of roads connected to Rockefeller's previously built roads. Although the new roads were officially ordered by Dorr, it was Rockefeller who studied and planned them, simply making "suggestions" as to where they might be placed.

Rockefeller financed these new roads with the condition that a new motor road also be constructed through the park. Although Rockefeller was hardly thrilled with the steady stream of automobiles pouring onto the island, he realized that they were inevitable and he wanted to plan for them wisely.

Rockefeller's proposed motor road immediately drew heat from the same small group of wealthy summer residents who opposed his carriage roads. Again it was George Pepper, by this time a Senator from Pennsylvania, who led the charge. Pepper contacted Secretary of the Interior Hubert Work and used his influence to halt construction of both the motor road and the new carriage roads. Pepper and others felt the new park was already drawing too many people to Mount Desert Island. A motor road, they argued, would only encourage more to come. Such feelings were summed up in a 1924 article in the *Boston Evening Transcript*: "Protests were especially emphatic from the view-point of many of the summer residents, who had long enjoyed the blissful quiet and primitive beauty of the island. They freely stated their fear that the proposed development would bring in a 'peanut crowd' of the Coney Island type, and that the park would speedily be littered with egg shells, banana peels, old tin cans."

> "When I thought a thing was worth doing, I made up my mind that the annoyances, the obstacles, the embarrassments had to be borne because the ultimate goal was worthwhile."
>
> —John D. Rockefeller, Jr.

Rockefeller saw things differently. As he had pointed out during a similar road building incident at another national park, "What are these parks for ...? The average American can't afford to go into the secluded areas or to have private trips into the parks. He must travel on such a highway. That's the whole point of the national park system." Rockefeller, ever the populist, believed in making the parks accessible for the common man, as well as the elderly and handicapped.

Rockefeller had the full support of year-round residents, who welcomed the flood of money that road construction and increased tourism would bring. With the backing of local residents and Maine politicians, Rockefeller and Dorr pushed hard to continue construction of both the motor road and the carriage roads. In the face of such strong opposition, Senator Pepper backed down. Shortly thereafter, the Secretary of the Interior came to the island to examine the situation firsthand. After viewing the roads, he concluded that they were indeed a worthy improvement. He gave his full blessing to the roads already under construction—with the stipulation that any future roads be approved by his office.

Emboldened by the overwhelming public support for his cause, Rockefeller charged ahead with plans for an even larger network of carriage roads and an expanded motor road. To bypass the approval demanded by Secretary Work, Rockefeller built new roads on land earmarked for (but not yet donated to) the park. Only when the roads were finished would the land be transferred to the park. Another round of protests erupted, but this time there was nothing that could be legally done to halt the construction.

By 1940 Rockefeller's grand vision was complete. A 57-mile network of carriage roads stretched from Bar Harbor to Seal Harbor, passing numerous mountains, lakes, and ponds. Curving gracefully through the woods, the roads revealed some of the park's most beautiful, hidden scenery. Every twist and turn was personally selected by Rockefeller, whose knowledge of road building and hands-on involvement in the undertaking were legendary. Rockefeller also commissioned 17 exquisite stone bridges along the carriage roads. Each bridge, unique in design, was handcrafted by stonemasons and financed by Rockefeller at extraordinary cost.

When all was said and done, Rockefeller had spent nearly 30 years and several million dollars building the carriage roads. When construction first began in 1913, horse-drawn carriage rides were still a popular aspect of island life. By 1940, however, they had turned into a quaint pastime for the rich. At the same time, bicycle use had taken off in America. Rockefeller was aware of this fact, and he was one of the first to encourage opening the carriage roads to bicycles. Today, bicycles are the most popular way to explore the carriage roads.

Following Rockefeller's death in 1960, the carriage roads fell into disrepair. To remedy the situation, the non-profit Friends of Acadia established a multimillion dollar endowment for the ongoing upkeep of the carriage roads. After several years of rehabilitation, Mr. Rockefeller's roads were restored to their full glory, and today they are as magnificent as ever.

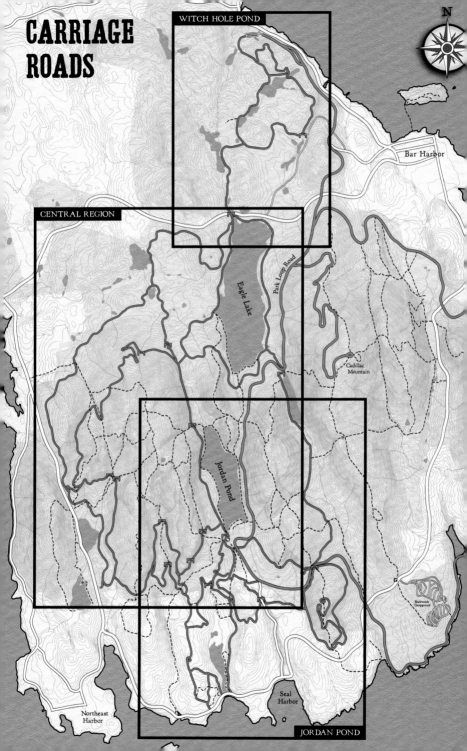

CENTRAL REGION

N

233

6
9

11

Eagle Lake

Park Loop Road

Seven
Bridges

8

7

Chasm Brook
Bridge

10

Bubble
Pond
Bridge

Bubble Pond

Sargent
Mtn.

North
Bubble

198
3

Parkman
Mtn.

Deer Brook
Bridge

South
Bubble

Pemetic
Mtn.

Hemlock
Bridge

Penobscot
Mtn.

Waterfall
Bridge

Jordan Pond

12

13

Upper
Hadlock
Pond

Amphitheater
Bridge

West
Branch
Bridge

14

Jordan Pond
House

15

16

20

Little
Harbor
Brook
Bridge

21

Cliffside
Bridge

23

25

Wildwood
Stables

18

19

Cobblestone
Bridge

24

26   29

Brown Mtn.
Gatehouse

22

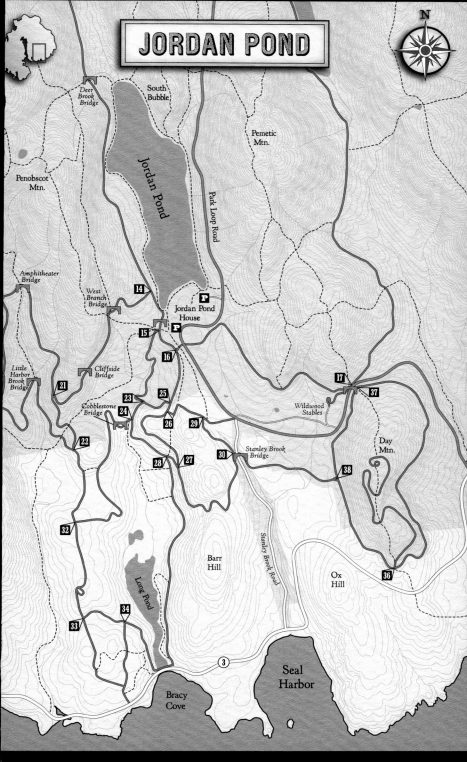

SCHOODIC PENINSULA

RUGGED, ROCKY SCHOODIC Peninsula juts out into the Gulf of Maine just east of Mount Desert Island, forming the only part of Acadia National Park connected to the mainland. The peninsula's 2,000 acres are surrounded by a craggy shore and covered in lush spruce-fir forest, but Schoodic has limited bragging rights when it comes to truly dramatic scenery. There are no towering mountains, hidden lakes, or sandy beaches here. What Schoodic does offer, however, is a gorgeous glimpse of raw, undeveloped Downeast Maine. What's more, its relatively remote location keeps it sheltered from the swarms of tourists that descend on Mount Desert Island each summer, giving Schoodic Peninsula a more subtle, peaceful charm. If crowded roads and screaming children are fraying your nerves, Schoodic might be the scenic Valium you need.

Although Schoodic Peninsula lies only five miles east of Mount Desert Island as the seabird flies, it's a little over an hour's drive (50 miles) by car along Route 1. Unless you're eager to explore some of the great restaurants and art galleries along Route 1, a better route to Schoodic is via the Bar Harbor Ferry (207-288-2984, www.barharborferry.com), which runs a water taxi between Bar Harbor and Winter Harbor, a small fishing village near the peninsula. In July and August the Island Explorer shuttle system also offers a Schoodic route that loops around the peninsula and passes through Winter Harbor. These days, visiting Schoodic Peninsula from Bar Harbor couldn't be easier.

Schoodic's one-way road makes a full loop around the Peninsula when combined with a short stretch of Route 186. Unlike Mount Desert Island's crowded Park Loop Road, the Schoodic Loop Road is relatively free of traffic, making it great for biking. And if you take the Bar Harbor Ferry to Winter Harbor, you can bring your bike along for an extra $5.

Schoodic Peninsula was added to the park in 1929. Prior to the addition, Acadia National Park was called Lafayette National Park. The original name was chosen in 1919 to reflect America's pro-French sentiment in the wake of World War I. Schoodic was later donated by three Anglophile sisters on the condition that the name of the park be changed to something less French. George Dorr, the park's first superintendant, suggested the name Acadia based on an early name for the region. Apparently unknown to the sisters, "Acadia" was based on *L'Acadie*, a name given by—*sacre bleu!*—the French.

MDI to Winter Harbor

If you're driving to Schoodic Peninsula from Mount Desert Island, follow Route 1A to Ellsworth, then turn right (east) on Route 1. This will take you to Route 186, which heads south to Winter Harbor and Schoodic Peninsula. There are a few pretty glimpses of the ocean along Route 1, but for the most part it's a ho-hum highway with plenty of auto shops and commercial businesses. That said, there are some interesting shops and artists galleries scattered along the way. If you like browsing art galleries, pick up a copy of the Artist Studio Tour Map, which is available in local stores. Lovers of specialty foods will enjoy Bartlett Estate Winery (175 Chicken Mill Pond Rd, 207-546-2408), which has been producing high-end fruit wines for over 20 years. Sullivan Harbor Smokehouse (207-422-3735) and Grindstone Neck of Maine (311 Newman St., 207-963-7347) also offer terrific smoked salmon and seafood.

RESTAURANTS

 Le Domaine (Din)
By far the best restaurant for miles, Le Domaine serves classic French cuisine in a charming dining room. (1515 Route 1, 207-422-3395)

Chester Pike's Galley (Brk, Lnch, Din on Fri & Sun)
This local favorite offers big portions at reasonable prices. (2236 Route 1, 207-422-8200)

Winter Harbor

This small fishing village (pop. 1,000) is home to lobstermen, whose boats dot the pretty harbor, and wealthy summer folk, whose giant mansions dot the shores of Grindstone Neck, the small peninsula at the eastern end of the harbor. Winter Harbor—so named because it was a popular place to shelter boats during fierce winter storms—is famous for its annual Lobster Festival, held the second Saturday in August. The highlight of the festival is the lobsterboat race, where locals race their lobsterboats at speeds topping 45 miles per hour. Locals take this competition so seriously that the race features 13 classes of lobsterboats.

RESTAURANTS

The Fisherman's Inn (Din)
This classic Downeast restaurant has been serving fresh seafood since 1947. Although the nautical decor is a bit uninspired, the food is fresh and well-prepared. (7 Newman Street, 207-963-5585)

Chase's (Brk, Lnch, Din)
This cheap, low-key diner serves all the classics (lobster roll, clam chowder) plus some inventive fare like lobster pesto omelettes. (193 Main Street, 207-963-7171)

Schoodic Peninsula

Continuing on Route 186 past Winter Harbor, you'll soon reach the well-marked turnoff to Schoodic Peninsula and the Schoodic Loop, a 6-mile one-way road that circumnavigates the peninsula. The road is two-way up to Frazier Point Picnic Area, after which it becomes one-way only. Keep in mind that parking is not permitted in the right lane of the road. There are, however, several pullouts where you can park and wander down to the shore.

FRAZIER POINT PICNIC AREA

This pretty little point (above) has about a dozen picnic tables scattered around a grassy knoll that gently slopes down to the shore. There are also fire rings, restrooms and drinking water. A small, wooden footbridge that juts into the cove is a nice place to take in the views. If you brought a bike, you can park your car here and follow the one-way road by bike.

WINTER HARBOR LIGHTHOUSE

As you continue along the road, you'll pass several clearings with views of rocky shores and cobblestone beaches. Across the harbor you'll see Winter Harbor Lighthouse, built on tiny four-acre Mark Island in 1856. The 19-foot tower was faithfully lit by nine keepers and their families until 1933, at which point the light was discontinued and replaced by a lighted buoy. The lighthouse then went into private ownership. It has since attracted a long string of literary types. Since 1933, no less than five writers have lived in the lighthouse.

RAVEN'S NEST
These steep, rugged cliffs offer some of Schoodic's most dramatic scenery. To find the unmarked trail that heads to the cliffs, drive 1.5 miles past Frazier Point and look for a small pullout on the left (just past a 35 mph sign on the right side of the road). The not-so-obvious trail passes over gnarled roots and heads to several dramatic drop-offs. Be extremely careful here. The footing is loose, the trails are faint, and the drop-offs are steep to the jagged shore below.

SCHOODIC HEAD
At 440 feet, Schoodic Head is the highest point on the peninsula. It's also home to one of Maine's largest stands of jack pine, a tree growing at the southern limit of its range. Although the views from the top are somewhat obscured by the vegetation, it still makes a fun side trip. About 2.5 miles past Frazier Point an unpaved road turns left off the main road and continues for about a mile to a small parking area. Four-wheel drive and high clearance are recommended.

SCHOODIC POINT
After passing the turnoff for the Schoodic Education and Research Center, you'll end up at the multi-tiered parking area at Schoodic Point. This is the southernmost tip of Schoodic Peninsula. Because it lies fully exposed to the open ocean, its rocky shore get pounded by powerful waves when storms kick up huge swells in the Gulf of Maine. On big wave days, the surf can be spectacular, but use caution! Rouge waves have swept spectators off the rocks here.

LITTLE MOOSE ISLAND
Continuing on the road past Schoodic Point, you'll see Little Moose Island on your right. This pretty little island is accessible by foot at low tide, but don't wander over without consulting a tide chart. If you don't pay attention to the rising tide, you can become stranded on the island until the next low tide.

BLUEBERRY HILL PARKING AREA
This tiny parking area is a great place to escape the crowds and enjoy nice views of Little Moose Island and Schoodic Island, which both protect nesting seabirds.

ANVIL TRAIL
This moderate hiking trail, which starts just north of the Blueberry Hill Parking Area, heads 1.1 miles to Schoodic Head. From Schoodic Head I like to make a loop back to the Blueberry Hill Parking Area by heading down the Schoodic Head Trail (0.6 miles) and the Alder Trail (0.6 miles).

SCHOODIC HARBOR & WONSQUEAK HARBOR
Continuing along the eastern edge of Schoodic Peninsula, you'll pass Schoodic Harbor and tiny Wonsqueak Harbor before exiting the park. Continue on the two-way road until you reach Birch Harbor, which intersects with Route 186.

Schoodic Point

ISLE AU HAUT

LOCATED 15 MILES southwest of Mount Desert Island, Isle au Haut is Acadia's most far-flung parcel of property. While Mount Desert Island is defined by tourism, Isle au Haut is a genuine working Maine island where fishing has been the primary occupation for over 200 years. Today about 65 people live year-round on the six mile long by two mile wide island. Roughly half of Isle au Haut belongs to Acadia National Park—representing arguably the most pristine coastal landscape in Maine. If "rugged," "remote," and "rock-bound" are some of your favorite words, it's time to add "Isle au Haut" to your vocabulary.

Isle au Haut ("High Island") was named by the French explorer Samuel Champlain in 1604. Although Champlain traveled up and down the coast of Maine on his voyage of discovery, he named very few places along the way. But Isle au Haut, with its tall mountains rising hundreds of feet above the water, was simply too obvious a landmark to remain anonymous. Not surprisingly, the island's high elevation makes it great for hiking. Over 18 miles of rugged trails crisscross the park. But other than hiking, relaxing and soaking in the scenery, there's not much else to do on Isle au Haut—which is exactly why some people love it.

Now the hard part: getting to Isle au Haut, which reaches farther into the Atlantic (15 miles) than any other large island in Maine. The first step is to drive to Deer Isle, an island six miles north of Isle au Haut that's connected to the mainland by a bridge. At the southern tip of Deer Isle is the town of Stonington (a two-hour drive from Bar Harbor) where you can catch the mailboat/passenger ferry to Isle au Haut. The cost is about $35 per person round-trip (first-come, first-served). You can also bring bikes and kayaks for an extra fee. Schedules vary depending on the season, but from mid-June to early September (except Sundays) the ferry also stops at Duck Harbor, located near the southern tip of the island. Contact the Isle au Haut Boat Company for current schedules and fares (207-367-5193, www.isleauhaut.com). Another option is Old Quarry Adventures, which offers hiking, biking, and kayaking day trips to Isle au Haut on the *Nigh Duck* (207-367-8977, www.oldquarry.com)

Day tripping to Isle au Haut (catching the morning and evening ferry) gives you about seven hours on the island. But it takes enough effort to get here that you might as well spend the night, giving you plenty of time to explore the island. There are two lodging options on Isle au Haut: cozy, expensive inns near the town landing, or rugged, inexpensive lean-to shelters at the park's Duck Harbor Campground. If you'd like to stay at an inn, visit www.jameskaiser.com for detailed, up-to-date hotel information. If you'd like to stay in a lean-to, follow the instruction on the following page.

TOWN LANDING

Isle au Haut's small town landing is the social hub of the island. It's also the best place to experience the slow pace of Maine island life. Just up the road is the Isle au Haut General Store (207-335-5211), which sells snacks and basic goods. Just down the road is Acadia National Park's Isle au Haut ranger station (207-335-5551). And about a mile from the town landing is the scrumptious Black Dinah Chocolatiers (207-335-5010), which serves coffee and distinctive chocolates with flavors like blueberry-black pepper and strawberry-balsamic. Black Dinah chocolates, which are homemade with local organic ingredients, have become wildly popular online and are shipped all over the U.S. (www.blackdinahchocolatiers.com)

Before Isle au Haut was settled by whites, Wabanaki Indians paddled to the island to gather sweetgrass and hunt ducks by driving them into the island's narrow harbor (now named Duck Harbor). The first white settler arrived in 1772, and fifty years later there were roughly 200 people living on Isle au Haut, most of them fishermen who benefitted from the island's close proximity to offshore fishing grounds. In 1860 a lobster cannery opened on the island, and by the 1880s roughly 300 people lived here. But when gas-powered engines arrived in the early 1900s, fishermen could commute from the mainland and Isle au Haut's population fell dramatically. Today there are roughly 65 year-round residents on Isle au Haut. Among the current locals: Linda Greenlaw, the female swordfish captain chronicled in *The Perfect Storm*, and the author of *The Hungry Ocean* and *The Lobster Chronicles*.

DUCK HARBOR CAMPGROUND

This small campground, operated by Acadia National Park, is home to five lean-to shelters that offer the only camping on Isle au Haut. Each 8-foot by 12-foot lean-to sleeps up to six people. Facilities include a fire ring, picnic table, and pit toilet. The campground is open from May 15 to October 15, and reservations are required prior to arrival. Contact the park for a reservation request form (207-288-3338) or go online at www.nps.gov/acad. One reservation covers camping for up to six people with a maximum stay of three to five nights. From Mon–Sat during peak season, the mailboat ferry stops at the landing in Duck Harbor, about a quarter mile from the campsite. Off season you'll have to hike five miles from the town landing to reach Duck Harbor Campground.

HIKING ON ISLE AU HAUT

Isle au Haut's best hiking trails are concentrated at the southern tip of the island, not far from Duck Harbor Campground. Among the most popular: Duck Harbor Mountain (Strenuous, 2.4 miles round-trip), which rises 300 feet above Duck Harbor. Another good option is connecting the Cliff Trail and Western Head Trail (Moderate, 2 miles one-way) which will take you in and out of dark spruce forests along Western Head. Although the trails on Isle au Haut are often rugged and overgrown, they're always worth it.

Kimball Island & Isle au Haut

BAR HARBOR

Filled with more shops, restaurants and hotels than all other towns on the island combined, Bar Harbor is the unofficial capital of Mount Desert Island. Its narrow streets and ramshackle buildings, perched on a gentle hill overlooking the harbor, make it the quintessential Maine Coastal Town. Ice cream shops, trinket stores, and the smell of fresh seafood round out the effect. To some it's a tourist trap. To others it's a vibrant slice of Downeast Maine. No matter what your take, chances are you'll end up in Bar Harbor at some point on your trip.

The heart of Bar Harbor is the T-intersection of Main Street and Cottage Street, located just up the hill from the town pier. Both streets are sardine-packed with shops and restaurants that offer a true study in contrasts: upscale galleries sell pricey artwork near novelty stores selling plastic lobsters; gourmet restaurants compete with greasy spoons; a Christmas store is located steps away from a biker shop selling bowie knives and ninja stars. It's hard to put your finger on the retail pulse of Bar Harbor, which means there's truly something for everyone here.

Equally incongruous is the social fabric of Bar Harbor. Fannypacked retirees, ragged hippies, Gore-tex clad outdoor buffs, casual fleece yuppies—all find fertile ground in Bar Harbor. There are also plenty of hard working locals, college party kids, and seasonal workers from foreign countries.

Although famous for its shops and restaurants, Bar Harbor is also the jumping off point for many of the island's most popular outdoor adventures—sea kayaking, whale watching, sailing cruises, etc. And if you want to explore Acadia's carriage roads, you can rent bikes in Bar Harbor and catch the free Island Explorer shuttle to Eagle Lake. The Bar Harbor Village Green, located in the center of town at the intersection of Main Street and Mount Desert Street, is the transportation hub for nearly all Island Explorer shuttles, which can take you just about anywhere on the island. And when rain puts the lid on outdoor fun, Bar Harbor's two movie theaters, multiple museums, and half dozen bars will keep you—and the rest of the island—entertained for hours.

During peak season in July and August, Bar Harbor is flooded with visitors—especially when cruise ships are in town. These days roughly 100 cruise ships call to port in Bar Harbor, up from 30 in 2000. Today Bar Harbor is the most popular port of call in Maine. On days when cruise ships disgorge hundreds of passengers onto the town's busy streets, long lines often form at popular shops and restaurants. If you happen to visit Bar Harbor when one (or two) enormous ships are in port, consider heading elsewhere and exploring Bar Harbor another day.

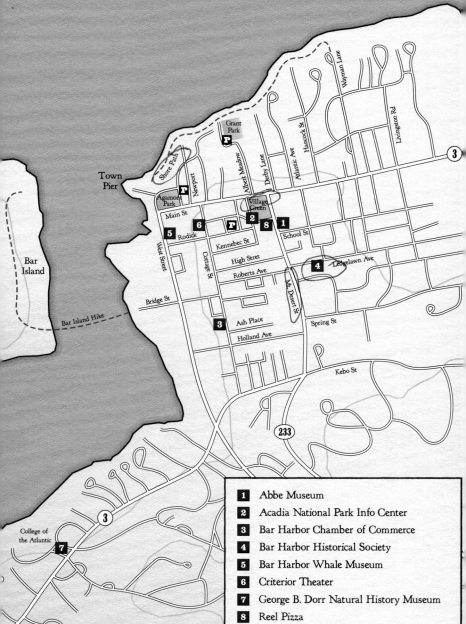

BAR HARBOR

N

3

Grant
Park

Town
Pier

Shore Path

Agamont
Park

Main St

Rodick

Newport

Albert Meadow

Derby Lane

Atlantic Ave

Hancock St

Wayman Lane

Livingston Rd

Village
Green

2

5

6

1

8

School St

West Street

Cottage St

Kennebec St

High Stret

Roberts Ave

Mt. Desert St

4

Ledgelawn Ave

Bar
Island

Bridge St

Bar Island Hike

3

Ash Place

Holland Ave

Spring St

Kebo St

233

3

College of
the Atlantic

7

1	Abbe Museum
2	Acadia National Park Info Center
3	Bar Harbor Chamber of Commerce
4	Bar Harbor Historical Society
5	Bar Harbor Whale Museum
6	Criterior Theater
7	George B. Dorr Natural History Museum
8	Reel Pizza

Bar Harbor Sights

★ BAR HARBOR SHOREPATH

This easy, ¾-mile path wraps around the eastern tip of Bar Harbor, offering ter- rific views of Frenchman Bay and the Porcupine Islands. (Note that sections of the Shore Path pass over private property, so please be respectful.) Start your stroll at the Bar Harbor town pier, and follow the paved path towards the Bar Harbor Inn. To your right you'll see two cannons, which were once stationed on Egg Rock Island to guard Frenchman Bay. Past the cannons lies the Bar Harbor Inn, which started out as the Reading Room Clubhouse in 1887. At the time it was a private, all-male "literary club" where "most of the reading was done through the bottom of a cocktail glass." Continue down the Shorepath and you'll see Balance Rock, a large, precariously balanced boulder that was carried here by glaciers during the last Ice Age. When the glaciers melted, Balance Rock settled into its unlikely position. Grant Park, a bit farther down on the left, is a nice place for a picnic. Near the end of the Shore Path, you'll see the Bar Harbor breakwater, a man-made stone wall that shelters Bar Harbor from large offshore waves. Local lore claims the breakwater was financed by J.P Morgan, so large waves wouldn't spill cocktails on his yacht when he visited Bar Harbor. When you reach the end of the Shorepath, you can retrace your steps back to the Town Pier, or turn right and follow Wayman Lane up to Main Street where there are lots of shops and restaurants.

AGAMONT PARK

This popular park, set on a gentle hill overlooking the shore, offers gorgeous views of Bar Harbor, the Porcupine Islands, and Frenchman Bay. The park's fountain was brought from Italy and dates to around 1600. If you're here on the Fourth of July, Agamont Park offers the best views in town of the fireworks.

VILLAGE GREEN

This large, central park hosts a variety of art and music festivals throughout the summer. On Mondays and Thursdays in July and August, the Bar Harbor Town Band offers free concerts at 8pm. The west side of the Village Green serves as the hub for the Island Explorer shuttle system.

WEST STREET

West Street is great for a short stroll if you'd like to see some of Bar Harbor's grand old mansions, many of which have been converted to inns. Follow West street away from the Bar Harbor Pier and you'll pass the elegant Bar Harbor Club, which is over 100 years old and was fully restored in 2008 after falling into disrepair for several decades. Continue past Bridge Street—which leads down to Bar Island—and follow West Street to the Maine Sea Coast Mission. This Christian organization offers free social services to Mainers who live year-round on eight offshore islands. The elegant brick building that serves as their headquarters was previously owned by the heirs to the Campbell Soup fortune.

Bar Island

No visit to Bar Harbor is complete without a visit to the town's namesake island. Twice a day when the tide goes out, an underwater sandbar is exposed that temporarily connects Bar Harbor to Bar Island. The sandbar starts at the end of Bridge Street, about a half mile west of the Bar Harbor town pier. There's roughly a three-hour window (90 minutes before and after low tide) when you can walk across the sand bar and explore Bar Island. A 0.5-mile path on the island heads to an overlook 120-feet above sea level that offers terrific views of Bar Harbor. The path starts at the southern tip of Bar Island, continues past a large field, then bears left on the way towards the overlook. (Plan on a 15 to 20 minute walk from the Sand Bar to the overlook). Be sure to check local papers for tide schedules before walking across to Bar Island.

Visitor Information

ACADIA NATIONAL PARK INFORMATION CENTER

This small brick building next to the Village Green is staffed with people who can answer questions about Acadia National Park and the Island Explorer shuttle system. You can also purchase park passes and pick up free park publications.

BAR HARBOR CHAMBER OF COMMERCE

If you have questions about local businesses or need to find last-minute lodging, head to the Chamber of Commerce. Open daily 8am–5pm summer, 8am–4:30pm weekdays off-season (93 Cottage Street, 207-288-5103, www.barharborinfo.com).

Museums

★ ABBE MUSEUM

This large, impressive museum explores Indian cultures and traditions in Maine. The museum layout follows a reverse timeline, which starts in the present and goes backwards in time. Tools, crafts and other cultural artifacts are displayed, as well as modern artwork by native artists. A small museum shop sells beautiful native baskets, traditional crafts, and a large selection of books. Educational programs, craft workshops, and archaeological field schools are also offered. Open daily, admission: $6 adults, $2 children (26 Mount Desert Street, 207-288-3519, www.abbemuseum.org)

★ BAR HARBOR WHALE MUSEUM

This wonderful museum, working in conjunction with Allied Whale (p.79), is devoted to whales and seals in the Gulf of Maine. There are interactive displays, a bioacoustic chamber that plays the calls of underwater animals, and full skeletons of humpback, minke and pilot whales hanging from the ceiling. The adjacent gift shop sells educational toys and has an outstanding selection of ocean-related books. Open daily June to October, free admission. Note: By the time you read this, the location may have changed due to construction of a new hotel; call ahead or ask around. (52 West Street, 207-288-0288, www.barharborwhalemuseum.org)

★ BAR HARBOR OCEANARIUM

Located about nine miles northwest of Bar Harbor on Route 3, the Bar Harbor Oceanarium is a bit out of the way, but definitely worth the trek. If you're interested in the fascinating lives of lobsters, this is the place to start. The Oceanarium features a lobster museum and lobster hatchery, where thousands of baby lobsters are nurtured from birth to be released into Maine waters. There's also a touch tank, marine exhibits, and an outdoor salt marsh walk. Open Mon–Sat, 9am–5pm, mid-May to late October. Admission: $12 adults, $7 children (Route 3, 207-288-5005, www.theoceanarium.com)

GEORGE B. DORR NATURAL HISTORY MUSEUM

Located on the campus of the College of the Atlantic (half a mile north of downtown Bar Harbor on Route 3), this small museum is devoted to the natural history of Mount Desert Island. The museum features exhibits on local animals and a touch tank filled with crabs, starfish, sea cucumbers and other intertidal creatures. The museum is open mid-June to Labor Day, 10am–5pm. Admission: $3.50 adults, $1 children (105 Eden Street, Route 3, 207-288-5395, www.coamuseum.org).

BAR HARBOR HISTORICAL SOCIETY

This small museum is a great place to learn more about Bar Harbor's opulent Cottage Era. Historic photos are the real draw, but the museum also offers a wealth of information on Bar Harbor. Open mid-June to mid-October, Monday–Saturday, 1pm–4pm. Free admission
(33 Ledgelawn Ave., 207-288-0000, www.barharborhistorical.org)

What's that Sound?

Every day at noon and 9pm, a booming sound blasts through the streets of Bar Harbor, momentarily frightening and confusing anyone near the Village Green. The sound comes from a powerful air horn located on top of the Bar Harbor Fire Station, next to the Village Green. A century ago the noon blast allowed people to synchronize their clocks, and the 9 pm blast alerted minors of a citywide curfew. Today it's mostly a tradition, although the horn is still used to notify villagers of school closures in the winter due to snow.

Boat Tours

Boat tours (p.29) are one of the highlights of any trip to Mount Desert Island. Listed below are the best boat tours departing from Bar Harbor.

★ STARFISH ENTERPRISE

Diver Ed's "Dive-In Theater Cruise" might be my favorite boat tour on the island. See page 30 for more details.

★ BAR HARBOR WHALE WATCH CO

Famous for their whale watching trips on the *Friendship V* (p.30), Bar Harbor Whale Watch offers other boat trips including Nature and Sightseeing, Lobster Fishing and Seal Watching, and a Lighthouse Tour that visits five nearby lights. Trips and times vary throughout the season, with the most trips available in July and August. Stop by their ticket office at 1 West street to buy tickets and see which trips are available at which times. (207-288-2386, www.barharborwhales.com)

★ MARGARET TODD

This classic four-masted schooner offers the most popular sailing trip in Bar Harbor. See page 31 for more details.

LULU

Fascinated by lobsters and lobstering? Sign up for a trip on the 42-foot Lulu, where Captain John Nicolai hauls up actual lobster traps, pulls out live lobsters, and spouts off countless lobster facts. Seal watching at Egg Rock is also part of the trip, as is plenty of colorful, local history. (207-963-2341, www.lululobsterboat.com)

CHRISSY

If you're looking for an intimate sailing experience on a small sailboat, check out the Chrissy, a 29-foot Friendship Sloop. This historic ship, built in 1910 for lobstering, offers 1.5 to 2 hour cruises around Frenchman Bay and the Porcupine Islands. She can accommodate up to six passengers, and group rates are available. (207-288-2373, www.downeastwindjammer.com)

MISS SAMANTHA

The 56-foot Miss Samantha offers naturalist-guided tours of Baker Island, the most remote of the Cranberry Isles (p.271). Along the way to Baker Island you'll pass much of the spectacular eastern shore of Mount Desert Island. (207-288-5374, www.barharborwhales.com)

ADA C. LORE

This historic Oyster schooner, built in 1923 to dredge oysters in Delaware Bay, departs daily from the Harborside Marina on sailing trips around Frenchman Bay and the Porcupine Islands. The Ada C. Lore can accommodate up to 49 passengers. (207-288-4585, www.downeastwindjammer.com)

Bus Tours

Two narrated driving tours of Acadia National Park depart daily from Bar Harbor. Although I prefer going at my own pace via the fee Island Explorer shuttle, these tours are good if you enjoy narrated tours or if you only have a limited time on the Island and want to see the most famous parts of the park.

ACADIA NATIONAL PARK TOURS

Acadia National Park Tours offers a 2.5-hour naturalist-narrated bus tour of Bar Harbor and Acadia National Park. Trips depart downtown Bar Harbor at 10am and 2pm, May–October. Price: $28 adults, $15 children. Tickets available at Testa's Restaurant, 53 Main Street. (207-288-0300, www.acadiatours.com).

OLI'S TROLLEY

Oli's offers narrated one-hour, and 2.5-hour tours through Bar Harbor and Acadia National Park in modern trolleys with an antique feel. Trips run from 10am to 3:30pm. Purchase tickets in the Oli's Trolley store at 1 West Street. Price: $20 adults, $10 children (866-987-6553, www.acadiaislandtours.com).

Scenic Flights

As stunning as Acadia is from the land and the sea, nothing puts the dramatic topography of Mount Desert Island into perspective like the view from the air. Two scenic flight operators fly out of the Trenton airport (a 20-minute drive from Bar Harbor and accessible via the Island Explorer). Flights generally run from 20 minutes to an hour, but the 45-minute Lighthouse Tours, which fly over five lighthouses, are by far the most popular. Prices vary with the cost of fuel, so call and inquire.

SCENIC FLIGHTS OF ACADIA

These Cesna flights offer the best value by far. Their office is located in the small shack next to the airport just south of the Trenton Market on Route 1A. (207-667-6527, www.scenicflightsofacadia.com)

ACADIA AIR TOURS

For a unique experience, fly around the island in a yellow Biplane (built in the late 1990s) or soar around the island on an engine-less glider. Acadia Air Tours has two offices: one in Bar Harbor at 1 West Street, and one near the airport just north of the Trenton Market. (207-667-7627, www.acadiaairtours.com)

Sea Kayaking

Bar Harbor is home to several of the best sea kayak outfitters on Mount Desert Island, which offer trips around Frenchman Bay as well as trips on the western "quiet side" of the island. See page 23 for detailed sea kayaking info.

Biking

Bar Harbor is home to two bicycle rental shops. Bike rentals are available for a half day or a full day.

BAR HARBOR BICYCLE SHOP

Since 1977 the Bar Harbor Bicycle Shop has been catering to casual tourists and hardcore bike enthusiasts. Open from March through December.
(141 Cottage Street, 207-288-3886, www.barharborbike.com)

ACADIA BIKE AND CANOE

In addition to renting bikes, Acadia Bike and Canoe offers organized biking trips on Mount Desert Island, Schoodic Peninsula, and Swan's Island. Multi-day bicycle tours are also available.
(48 Cottage Street, 207-288-9605, www.acadiabike.com)

Golf

KEBO VALLEY GOLF CLUB

Bar Harbor's 18-hole Kebo Valley Golf Club, founded in 1888, is the eighth oldest golf course in America and the best golf course on Mount Desert Island.
(100 Eagle Lake Road, 207-288-5000, www.kebovalleyclub.com)

Notable Stores

BAR HARBOR BREWING COMPANY

This terrific brewing company (p.50) offers free tastings throughout the day at their downtown store. In addition to beer, they also sell local sodas and wines.
(8 Mount Desert Street, 207-288-4592)

SHERMAN'S BOOKSTORE

Sherman's is the largest bookstore on the island, with a terrific selection of books about Acadia and Downeast Maine, plus plenty of popular fiction, nonfiction and children's books. (56 Main Street, 207-288-3161)

CADILLAC MOUNTAIN SPORTS

If you're looking for outdoor gear, look no further than Cadillac Mountain Sports, which has the best selection on the island. (26 Cottage Street, 207-288-4532)

J.H. BUTTERFIELD CO.

This specialty grocery store has a large selection of wine, beer and gourmet foods. There's also a great selection of local items like blueberry jam and maple syrup.
(152 Main Street, 207-288-3386)

Entertainment

CRITERION THEATER
This historic art-deco theater, open since 1932, plays big Hollywood films and occasionally features live comedy or music. The theater is a bit faded, but that's part of its charm. Balcony seats upstairs are definitely worth the extra dollar in ticket price. (35 Cottage Street, 207-288-3441, www.criteriontheater.com)

REEL PIZZA
This two-screen theater shows a mix of big Hollywood films and small independent and foreign films. Best of all, there are couches and recliners, and they sell fresh pizza and beer. (33 Kennebec Place, 207-288-3811, www.reelpizza.com)

IMPROVACADIA
This improv comedy troupe, founded by the former music director of Chicago's legendary Second City, performs live nightly. As with all improv, performances vary, but every time I've gone the $15 has been worth the price of admission. (15 Cottage St., 2nd Floor, 207-288-2503)

Groceries
The largest grocery store in town is **Hannaford** (86 Cottage Street, 207-288-5680). There are also two small natural food stores: **A&B Naturals** (101 Cottage Street, 207-288-8480) and **The Alternative** (16 Mount Desert Street, 207-288-8225). You can also buy farm-fresh food at the weekly **Bar Harbor Farmer's Market**, held every Sunday from 10am–2pm in the YMCA parking lot (21 Park Street).

Nightlife
Bar Harbor has the liveliest nightlife on the island with roughly half a dozen popular bars. At every bar you can expect a casual vibe, no dress code, and cocktails served in pint glasses. The liveliest spot in town is **Carmen Verandah**, which serves up nightly dance parties fueled by bands and DJs. Just below Carmen Verandah you'll find the always popular **Rupununi** and **Joe's Smoke Shop**. The **Dog and Pony**, located behind the Fire Station, features an outdoor patio that pulls a lively, diverse crowd on hot summer nights. Down the street is the funky **Lompoc Cafe**, which is popular with local hippies and hipsters. On Cottage Street you'll find the **Thirsty Whale**, a classic pub with great bar food, and **Leary's Landing**, a tiny Irish Bar that gets packed in the summer. If you're looking for a beer but don't want to be surrounded by drunk 20-somethings, head down the road to the **Black Friar Pub**, a mellow English-style pub that's located on the first floor of the Black Friar Inn. If you're looking for a sports bar filled with big screen TVs, head to **Little Anthony's** at the far end of Cottage Street.

BAR HARBOR

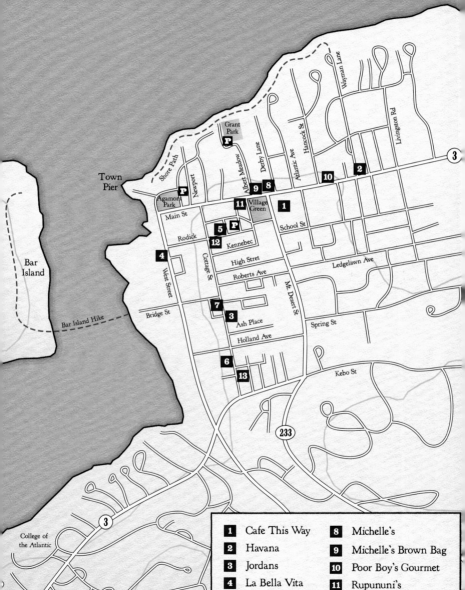

N

Town
Pier

Grant
Park

Shore Path

Agamont
Park

Main St

Rodick

Bar
Island

Bar Island Hike

West Street

Cottage St

Bridge St

Newport
Albert Meadow
Derby Lane

Village
Green

Kennebec

High Street

Roberts Ave

Ash Place

Holland Ave

Atlantic Ave

Hancock St

Wayman Lane

Livingston Rd

School St

Ledgelawn Ave

Mt. Desert St

Spring St

Kebo St

233

3

College of
the Atlantic

3

1 Cafe This Way

2 Havana

3 Jordans

4 La Bella Vita

5 Lompoc Cafe

6 Mache

7 Maggie's

8 Michelle's

9 Michelle's Brown Bag

10 Poor Boy's Gourmet

11 Rupununi's

12 Rosalie's Pizza

13 Two Cats

Bar Harbor Restaurants

★ MÂCHE (Din: $20–26)

This small French-style bistro is my favorite restaurant in downtown Bar Harbor. The menu changes frequently, but expect bold flavors from dishes like Filet au Poivre and Duck Cassoulet. The appetizers ($9–12) are so good you could make a superb tapas-style meal. The atmosphere is sophisticated, the wine list is superb, and the desserts are decadent. (135 Cottage Street, 207-288-0447)

★ BURNING TREE (Din: $22–28)

This cozy, hip restaurant offers creative cuisine that combines flavors from around the world with plenty of local ingredients (many of the herbs and vegetables come from their own garden) The extensive menu always has plenty of interesting seafood, which is artfully and exquisitely prepared. (Located five miles south of Bar Harbor on Route 3. Closed Tuesdays. 207-288-9331)

★ MICHELLE'S FINE DINING (Brk: $8–10, Din: $26-38)

Traditional French cuisine with a New England flair. Located in the charming Ivy Manor Inn, Michelle's is the most formal and elegant restaurant in Bar Harbor, serving up old-school classics like Beef Wellington with an expert touch. Perfect for a romantic meal or a special occasion. Good wine list. If you're a serious foodie, ask about their exclusive "Chef's Table". (194 Main Street, 207 288 2138)

★ MAGGIE'S (Din: $16–24)

If you're the type who avoids "trendy" restaurants in favor of those that simply focus on quality ingredients and skilled preparation, Maggie's is for you. They grow their own produce, buy local meat and seafood, and prepare everything from scratch. Their lobster crêpes with French brandy sauce might be the best lobster dish on the island. (6 Summer Street, 207-288-9007)

★ LA BELLA VITA (Brk: $8–11, Lnch, Din: $8–26)

This upscale Italian restaurant, located in the elegant Harborside Hotel, offers the best Italian food on the island. Many breakfast items are prepared with an Italian touch, and the Lunch and Dinner menu features focaccia and panini sandwiches ($8–11) and Italian classics like veal scallopini and chicken piccata ($22–26). The cozy dining room features nice views of the harbor. (55 West Street, 207-288-5033)

CAFE THIS WAY (Brk: $7–9, Din: $21-28)

Creative, adventurous cuisine in a laid-back atmosphere. The breakfast menu is extensive and offers up all the classics with plenty of foodie flair. Dinners run the gamut from steak to tofu, all uniquely prepared (duck wrapped scallops, tempura ahi tuna, tempeh with bbq sauce). Good wine list and creative cocktails. (14 1/2 Mount Desert St, 207-288-4483)

Best Bar Harbor Restaurants

Best Breakfast: Cafe This Way, 2 Cats, Michelle's

Best Seafood: Burning Tree, Maggie's

Best to Impress: Mache, Michelle's

Best Value: Michelle's Brown Bag Cafe, Rosalie's

Best Deserts: Poor Boys Gourmet

HAVANA (Din: $24-32)

"Nuevo Latino" cuisine in a hip, upscale setting. Havana offers plenty of local food prepared with Latin flair (Jerked Scallops and Shrimp, Pulled Pork Mole, Paella). There's an impressive wine list, plus mojitos, caiparinas and other south-of-the-border cocktails. (318 Main Street, 207-288-2822)

POOR BOY'S GOURMET (Din: $14-22)

Poor Boy's is popular for its traditional food (Baked Stuffed Haddock, Chicken Parmigiana), spectacular desserts (Jack Daniels Chocolate Pecan Pie, Bailey's White Chocolate Cheesecake), and $10 Early Bird specials between 4:30 and 6:00. The atmosphere is comfortable and relaxed, and the menu has plenty of lobster entrees that don't require bibs or cracking utensils. (300 Main Street, 207-288-4148)

ROSALIE'S PIZZA (Din: $6-15)

Arguably the best pizza in Maine. In a town where it's easy to spend $100 on dinner for two, Rosalie's remains a superb value, especially for families. Fresh, quality ingredients and homemade dough make all the difference. They also offer subs, calzones, stuffed slices and salads. (46 Cottage Street, 207-288-5666)

TWO CATS (Brk: $8-10)

One of the best breakfast spots in town with a strong emphasis on quality ingredients. Famous for their eggs Benedict, served on homemade biscuits with a side of spicy home fries. Located in a renovated home, the interior is cozy and hip. There's almost always a wait, but reservations are accepted. Open till 1pm daily. (130 Cottage Street, 207-288-2808)

MICHELLE'S BROWN BAG CAFE (Brk, Lnch: $7-9)

Hands down the best sandwich shop in town (It's the same owner as Michelle's fine dining). Classic sandwiches with top-notch ingredients, plus foccacia paninis and tasty soups and salads. Perfect for take-out. (156 Main Street, 207-288-5858)

LOMPOC CAFE (Lnch, Din: $8–18)

This bar/restaurant serves upscale comfort food and a great selection of local microbrews. The menu features sandwiches and burgers ($8–9) as well as more substantial entrees ($14–18). Their outdoor patio and bocce court are always popular with the local hippie/hipster crowd. (36 Rodick Street, 207-288-9392)

RUPUNUNI'S (Lnch, Din: $8–24)

If you're looking for a good sit-down lunch, Rupununi's combines upscale, bistro-style food (burgers: $8, pasta & seafood: $16–24) with a full bar and an outdoor patio that offers the best people-watching in town. This is always one of the liveliest dinner spots in town. (119 Main Street, 207-288-2886)

JORDANS (Brk, Lnch: $4–8)

One of Bar Harbor's classic breakfast destinations. Open since 1976, Jordans is where the locals go to meet up with friends, catch up on gossip, and fill up on blueberry pancakes. Bursting with small town charm, eating at Jordan's feels like stepping into a Norman Rockwell painting. Open 5am–1pm, everyday. (80 Cottage Street, 207-288-3586)

Lobster In Bar Harbor

Unfortunately, there's no authentic lobster shack (p.48) in Bar Harbor, just several tourist versions that claim to charge "market price" for lobsters. (Don't believe it—when lobster prices collapsed in 2009, the "market price" charged by many Bar Harbor restaurants didn't budge from the historic highs set a few years earlier). That said, if you don't mind paying extra there are several waterfront restaurants where you can enjoy fresh lobster as you watch the lobstermen unload their catch. The best views in town are at the **Terrace Grille** (Lnch, Din: $9–22, 207-288-3351), an upscale outdoor restaurant situated on the lawn in front of the gorgeous Bar Harbor Inn. The **Fish House Grille** (Lnch, Din: $8–23, 207-288-3070), located next to the Bar Harbor Pier, is a classic seafood joint with baked and fried entrees, seafood rolls, chowder and a raw bar. And **Stewman's** (Lnch, Din: $9–22, 207-288-9723), situated on a pier jutting into the harbor, offers the best impression of a lobster shack in town. If you don't mind not being waterfront, check out **West Street Cafe** (Lnch, Din: $7–18, 207-288-5242), where you won't pay waterfront prices. And the best lobster *value* in town is the lobster roll at the scrappy **Main Street Market** (317 Main Street, 207-288-8185), which is fresh, cheap, and served on a non-traditional yet highly utilitarian hamburger bun.

SEAL HARBOR

SEAL HARBOR IS a tiny village with few tourist attractions—and its ultra-wealthy residents would like to keep it that way. Ox Hill, which rises above the eastern shore of Seal Harbor, is home to some of the most expensive homes in New England. But drive along its twisty roads and all you'll see are tiny wooden signs (painted in patented "Seal Harbor Green") proclaiming the oddly elegant names of the mansions lying at the end of the long, long driveways. *Felsmere, Keewaydin, Glengariff*—when it comes to Seal Harbor mansion names, the more *Lord of the Rings* the better. Meanwhile, down on Main Street, high-priced shops and boutiques are conspicuously absent from a town that boasts a greater net worth than many developing countries. And such tourist-luring establishments are unlikely to arrive anytime soon.

Although Seal Harbor is one of the wealthiest summer colonies in America, it remains relatively unknown because its residents come here to *escape* the spotlight. Seal Harbor is about getting back to nature—albeit from the comfort of 30-room mansions and 60-foot yachts. And therein lies the old-school, Old Money ethos of the town. Despite the throngs of private servants, private gardeners, and private assistants roaming Ox Hill in the summer, your average Seal Harbor millionaire is as apt to ramble on about native plants and migrating birds as hedge funds and currency swaps. This attitude is perhaps best embodied by the Rockefellers, who are actively involved with local charities and land conservation efforts.

But while Seal Harbor is known (or not known) for its stealth wealth, the town's otherwise low profile was thrust into the limelight with the arrival of Martha Stewart in 1997. After purchasing *Skylands*, a sprawling hilltop estate once owned by the Ford family, Martha dazzled her fans with glossy magazine spreads of her new summer hideaway. Suddenly, domestic divas everywhere knew that Seal Harbor was the *real* place to be in Maine. But despite the temporary commotion, the horsey-set residents simply hunkered down and let the commotion pass, and today the tiny village remains as charming and lackluster as ever.

In fact, Seal Harbor is probably the most under-appreciated town on the island. Most visitors simply drive by with little more than a passing glimpse of the picture perfect-harbor filled with expensive yachts. But Seal Harbor's tiny town green and jewel-like beach are great places to avoid the crowds and soak in the scenery. And Little Long Pond, just west of town, is a great place to stroll around and enjoy some dramatic mountain views.

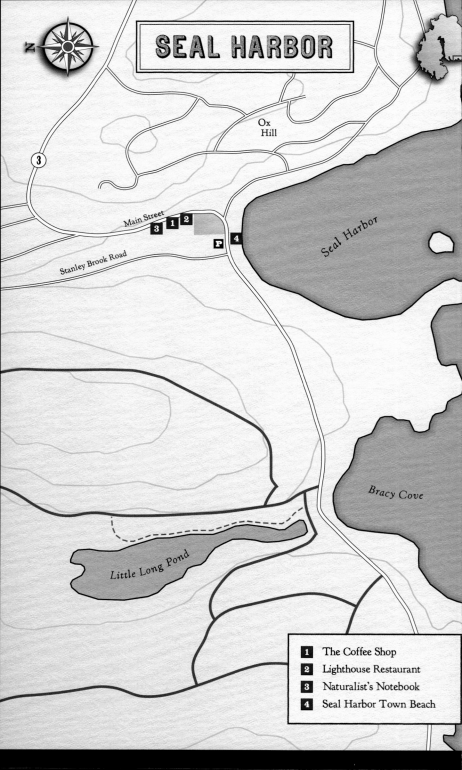

SEAL HARBOR

N

Ox
Hill

3

Main Street

3 1 2

P 4

Stanley Brook Road

Seal Harbor

Bracy Cove

Little Long Pond

1	The Coffee Shop
2	Lighthouse Restaurant
3	Naturalist's Notebook
4	Seal Harbor Town Beach

★ SEAL HARBOR TOWN BEACH
This small public beach is one of only two natural sand beaches on the island (the other is Sand Beach on the Park Loop Road). But while Sand Beach is often swarming with crowds on hot summer days, the Seal Harbor Town Beach generally stays quiet and relaxed. Even better, the ocean water in this shallow harbor is slightly—*slightly*—warmer than the water at Sand Beach.

NATURALIST'S NOTEBOOK
This charming store/museum is a nature-lover's dream come true. Inside you'll find books, photos, specimens, art displays, and ecologically friendly products spread across two floors. Open 10–5 daily. (16 Main Street, 207-801-2777)

LIGHTHOUSE RESTAURANT (Lnch: $9–12, Din: $17–22)
Seal Harbor's only restaurant boasts 1970s nautical decor and a menu to match, with lots of old-school seafood options. (12 Main Street, 207-276-3958)

THE COFFEE SHOP
This small cafe, located next to the Lighthouse Restaurant, sells coffee and espresso drinks, plus breakfast burritos and homemade pastries. Open 6am–4pm.

LITTLE LONG POND
This gorgeous pond lies just west of "downtown" Seal Harbor along Route 3. The low-key setting is a great place to kick back, relax and soak in the views of the mountains.

NORTHEAST HARBOR

IF SEAL HARBOR is a town of stealth wealth, Northeast Harbor is becoming a town of wealth on prominent display—to the consternation of the Old Money families that have summered here for generations. There once was a time when the Rockefellers, Astors and Fords drove around Northeast Harbor in beat-up automobiles, hobnobbed with locals, wore tattered clothes, and otherwise pretended that they were not, in fact, worth millions of dollars. But in the past few decades, New Money has slowly crept in, bringing bigger yachts, fancier cars, and other forms of conspicuous wealth to prove that they are, in fact, worth millions of dollars.

A few years back *W* magazine ran a profile of Northeast Harbor titled "The Wasps Nest." Fear swept over some summer residents that their Old Money hideaway had finally been exposed. The thought of Mount Desert Island ever becoming the next Martha's Vineyard or, worse, *The Hamptons*, had many blue bloods coughing up cheap grilled cheese sandwiches at the ultra-exclusive Northeast Harbor Swim Club (where the food served is *soooo* not New Money). But to date, P. Diddy has yet to motor into the harbor and pop open a bottle of Cristal. And despite the unsavory influx of a few billionaires who actually earned their money, Northeast Harbor appears to be hanging on to its relatively low-key profile just fine. Old Money types still spend their days thumbing through the prestigious "Redbook"—a tiny, secretive directory listing the winter and summer addresses of the Northeast Harbor/Seal Harbor elite—and private clubs still have decades-long "waiting lists" for new members wishing to apply.

But despite the private drives, private clubs, and other private enclaves, Northeast Harbor remains a fabulous place to visit. And some of its top attractions are—hold your breath—free! Which is not to say you should leave your credit card at home. Main Street is filled with pricey art galleries and other high-end shops catering to gourmet tastes, so plan accordingly.

Ironically, Northeast Harbor was born of rather humble circumstances. In the early 1800s it was home to farmers and fishermen. The first summer visitors consisted of artists, clergymen and intellectuals. When a wealthy New York banker offered to buy a Northeast Harbor farmer's property in the late 1800s, the farmer responded, "We have some very fine people in Northeast Harbor, including a Bishop and three college Presidents. We don't want any Wall Street riffraff!" My how times have changed.

Northeast Harbor Sights

★ THUYA GARDEN & LODGE

Perched on a hill above Northeast Harbor, Thuya Garden is one of the most beautiful gardens on Mount Desert Island. You can drive to the garden via Thuya Drive, but I prefer hiking the moderate, ¼-mile trail that starts by the parking area just south of the Asticou Inn. The trail rises through a shady, pine-scented forest with views of the boat-filled harbor below. Thuya garden is a late summer garden that features spectacular blooms in August. Adjacent to the garden is Thuya Lodge, the former summer home of Joseph Curtis. The lodge has been kept exactly as Curtis left it, offering a rare glimpse into the lifestyles of early summer residents who, though wealthy, preferred the rustic life, thus earning them the name "Rusticators."

★ ART GALLERIES

Northeast Harbor is home to the best art galleries on the island, almost all of which are located along Main Street. Simply start at one of end Main Street and pop in wherever strikes your fancy.

★ SARGENT DRIVE

If you're heading back to Bar Harbor (or to the western side of the island), drive up beautiful Sargent Drive instead of boring Route 198. From downtown Northeast Harbor, drive down to South Shore Road, then cut across to Sargent Drive and follow it north past million dollar mansions and stunning views of Somes Sound.

BOAT TOURS

A small booth next to the harbormaster's office sells tickets and provides info for boat tours departing from Northeast Harbor, including ferry service to the Cranberry Isles. The *Sea Princess* offers nature cruises, historic cruises, and evening trips to the Islesford Dock Restaurant. (207-276-5352, www.barharborcruises.com) Downeast Friendship Sloop (www.sailacadia.com) offers sailboat trips for up to six people on the elegant Friendship Sloop *Helen Brooks*.

ASTICOU AZALEA GARDEN

This small, impeccably maintained garden features over 70 varieties of azaleas, laurels and rhododendrons. Different flowers bloom between late May and July, but the most impressive blooms generally happen in the first two weeks of June. The garden, designed by Northeast Harbor resident Charles K. Savage in 1956 and funded by John D. Rockefeller, Jr., is styled after a Japanese stroll garden. It even has a rock garden complete with raked sand. Open from May to November, sunrise to sunset. A small parking area is located off Route 198, just north of the intersection with Route 3.

NORTHEAST HARBOR TOWN DOCK

If you like looking at multi-million dollar sailboats and yachts, a stroll down to the town dock is a must. This is one of the best places in the world to see Hinckleys (p.261) in their native habitat. The yachts in the harbor are most impressive in July and August, before they've been put in storage or shipped down to Florida.

GREAT HARBOR MARITIME MUSEUM

With so many boat buffs in Northeast Harbor, it's no surprise that the town has the island's best maritime museum. Although small, the museum always has some interesting exhibits, which change from year to year. Open Tues–Sat, 10–5, late June to mid-September. (125 Main Street, 207-276-5262).

THE OLD SCHOOL HOUSE & MUSEUM

This small museum, located a short drive from Northeast Harbor on Route 198, is run by the Mount Desert Island Historical Society. Exhibits change, but they always focus on interesting aspects of Mount Desert Island's history. The yellow building, originally built as a schoolhouse in 1892, was restored by the Historical Society in 1999. (373 Sound Drive, 207-276-9323)

PETITE PLAISANCE

Petit Plaisance is the former home of French novelist Marguerite Yourcenar, the first woman inducted as an "immortal" into the Academie Francaise (the highest honor a writer can receive in France). When World War II broke out, Yourcenar fled to Northeast Harbor. Once here she decided she could never live anywhere else. Free tours in English or French are given by appointment between June 15–August 31 (South Shore Road, 207-276-3940).

Northeast Harbor Restaurants

★ REDBIRD PROVISIONS (Lnch $9-20, Din $24-35)

This casually fabulous restaurant mixes local, artisinal foods with Italian flavors and Asian spices. The decor is country chic, and the menu is dotted with foodie-rific ingredients like squash blossoms, fennel pollen and black trumpet mushrooms. FYI - the "Provisions" part of the name is more than just wordplay—they actually deliver ready-made, gourmet meals to the private homes and yachts in and around Northeast Harbor. (207-276-3006, 11 Sea Street)

★ BASSA COCINA DE TAPEO (Din: $20-30)

This hip, upscale restaurant offers small tapas ($8–13) and larger entrees ($20–30), with plenty of fresh, local seafood. Many tapas have Mediterranean flavors, and entrees often include classics like paella, oso buco and beef wellington. The wine list is good and deserts are a delight. (207-276-0555, 3 Old Firehouse Lane)

ASTICOU INN (Brk: $7–10, Lnch: $10–13, Din: $22–32)

Perched on a hill overlooking the harbor, this historic hotel (the oldest on the island, built in 1883) offers breakfast, lunch and dinner to the public. The food and decor are best described as rustic blue blood. Needless to say, if you're looking to soak in a bit of historic Northeast Harbor elegance, there's no better place. (207-276-3344, 15 Peabody Drive)

FULL BELLI DELI (Brk, Lnch: $7–9)

This great, reasonably-priced deli serves the best sandwiches in town. Tasty toppings include caramelized onions, cranberry relish and roasted red peppers. There are also salads, soups, baked goods and sides like coleslaw and potato salad, and a coffee bar with espresso drinks. (207-276-4299, 5 Sea Street)

COLONEL'S RESTAURANT (Brk: $7–8, Lnch, Din: $8–19)

If you're looking for something hearty and reasonably priced, check out this relaxed restaurant, which serves sandwiches and burgers ($8-11) and classic seafood entrees ($14-19). There are soups and salads, and the attached bakery sells breads and pastries. A full bar offers several beers on tap. (207-276-5147, 143 Main Street)

THE DOCKSIDER (Lnch, Din: $7–20)

For over 30 years, the Docksider has been serving burgers and sandwiches ($7–9) and seafood dinners ($13–20) on paper plates from a small, unassuming shack. If you're expecting an elegant meal, head elsewhere. If you'd like an old-school slice of ramshackle Downeast Maine, place your order at the window. Their lobster roll is overflowing with fresh lobster meat—and priced accordingly. (207-276-3965, 14 Sea Street)

Bear Island Lighthouse

This picturesque lighthouse, located on tiny Bear Island just off Northeast Harbor, first went into operation in 1839. The 31-foot tall brick tower is situated on the island's highest point and the beacon can be seen up to 10 miles away. Sadly, in the early 1980s the lighthouse was decommissioned and fell into disrepair. In 1987 Acadia National Park acquired the island, and in 1989 Friends of Acadia refurbished the lighthouse and the beacon was relit. To help pay for the upkeep of the lighthouse, the park service leases the island to a private individual who has a house on the far side of the island.

SOMESVILLE

SOMESVILLE IS SO quaint it hurts. The white clapboard houses, leafy side-walks, consistently friendly citizens, and impeccably well-tended flower beds seem to have sprung forth from a Norman Rockwell painting. But this is the real deal, complete with a Strawberry Festival in July, a Blueberry Festival in August, and Wednesday morning pie sales at the Somesville Union Meeting House. Simply put, Somesville is the kind of town where even thinking about swearing as you walk down the street makes you feel guilty.

Driving down Route 102, traveling at the posted speed limit of 35 mph, you can pass through Somesville in a little under a minute. Blink and you might miss it. But you'll know you're here when you see a gorgeous arched footbridge on the right side of the road—one of the most famous landmarks on the island. Almost all of the town's attractions are located within walking distance of the footbridge, so look for parking as soon as you see it (or use the Island Explorer shuttle, which will stop in Somesville on its way to Southwest Harbor if you ask).

Somesville was the first permanent town on Mount Desert Island. In 1761, 22-year-old Abraham Somes sailed north from Gloucester, Massachusetts, and built a log cabin on the shore of this well-protected harbor. The location offered plenty of oak trees (perfect for lumber), several nearby streams (perfect for hydro-power), and a saltwater marsh (perfect for hay). The following year Somes returned with his wife and three daughters and named the town "Betwixt the Hills." Before long several other families had joined them. By the 1830s Somesville had grown by leaps and bounds. According to one early report it had "one small store, one blacksmith shop, one shoemaker's shop, one tan-yard, two shipyards, one bark mill, one saw mill, one lath mill, one shingle mill, one grist mill, and one schoolhouse."

Two decades later, the town played a critical role in establishing Mount Desert Island as a major tourist destination. In the summer of 1855, Somesville hosted a large group of early tourists who spent a month at a local tavern. One of the tourists was Frederic Church, a famous artist whose paintings of Mount Desert Island catapulted the island to national fame. But within a few decades Somesville was no longer the most important town on Mount Desert Island. Bar Harbor and Southwest Harbor, which lay closer to coastal shipping routes, had become the island's new power centers, leaving Somesville high and dry. Development in Somesville ground to a halt, pickling the town in a colonial time warp that's perfect for modern-day sightseers.

(Note: This section also includes information on the nearby towns of Town Hill, Pretty Marsh, and Seal Cove.)

SOMESVILLE

N

102

198

Somes Harbor

Oak Hill Road

1 P

Somes
Pond

Pretty Marsh Rd

2

To Seal Cove
Auto Museum

Beech Hill Rd

102

1 Mount Desert Island Historical Society
2 Acadia Repertory Theater

Beech Hill Cross

★ SEAL COVE AUTO MUSEUM

Antique cars don't pop to mind when you think about Mount Desert Island, but the island is home to one of the most extraordinary antique car collections in the world. Thank summer resident Richard Paine, who inherited a fortune and spent much of it on classic cars. Before passing away, Paine set up a foundation to display his collection in perpetuity. There are five Model Ts, as well as Cadillacs, Buicks, and Benzes over 100 years old! (207-244-9242, 1414 Tremont Road)

FOOTBRIDGE AND MDI HISTORICAL SOCIETY

The Somesville footbridge is one of the most recognizable sights on the island. The small museum, located next to the footbridge, features changing exhibits on the history of Mount Desert Island. Alongside the museum is an heirloom garden that blooms from late May to October. (207-276-9323, www.mdihistory.org)

PRETTY MARSH

If you're looking for peace and quiet, check out this forested picnic area, set on a hill that slopes down to the shore. Due to its far-flung location, few visitors ever make it here, but its western exposure is great for sunsets (without the crowds!).

ACADIA REPERTORY THEATER

Since 1973 this professional theater company has been performing live plays in Somesville's rustic Masonic Hall. Between July and September they offer a good mix of comedies, dramas, children's plays and Agatha Christie murder mysteries. Reservations are recommended. (207-244-7260, www.acadiarep.com)

Restaurants

★ TOWN HILL BISTRO (Din:: $17-20)

Gourmet cuisine in a cozy, rustic atmosphere. Even though it's located in the middle of nowhere, savvy locals drive out of their way to eat here. The menu changes frequently, but gourmet cheese plates, chilled beet-raspberry soup, and homemade gnocchi are staples. Count on plenty of top-notch local ingredients. Reservations recommended. (1317 State Highway 102, 207-288-1011)

★ MOTHER'S KITCHEN (Brk, Lnch: $7-8)

Mother's Kitchen offers the best sandwiches on the island. It's easy to drive past this tiny shack on Route 198, but to do so would be a crime against gastronomy. Order a classic sandwich or get creative with ingredients like marinated steak, brie, roasted eggplant, or pesto mayo. If you like meatloaf sandwiches, try the Grandpa Jack. They also sell homemade pies, muffins, and specialty desserts. (Route 102 next to Salisbury Hardware, 207-288-4403)

SOUTHWEST HARBOR

SOUTHWEST HARBOR IS the largest town on the western "quiet" side of Mount Desert Island. Centered around a beautiful working harbor, it's a delightful mix of the island's three common human species: modest fishermen (mostly found in Bass Harbor), rich summer folk (mostly huddled together in Northeast and Seal Harbor), and vacationing tourists (drawn to Bar Harbor like moths to a flame). As such, you won't be hit over the head with an abundance of tourist options in Southwest Harbor, but that's all part of its charm.

That said, there's still plenty here to keep you occupied. Several boat tours depart from the harbor, and some of the island's best hikes are just a short drive away. Southwest Harbor is also home to some great B&Bs and some truly terrific restaurants. If you don't mind being a 30-minute drive away from the famous eastern side of the island—or you aren't thrilled about the crowds you'll encounter there in July and August—this is the place for you.

Due to its physical separation from the rest of the island, Southwest Harbor has always had a different vibe. It was the first town on the island to lift the famous automobile ban imposed by summer residents in the early 1900s, and today it revels in being more laid back than its exclusive neighbors across the way. The island's boozy Oktoberfest, featuring over 20 Maine microbreweries, is held here each year, and the town's annual Flamingo Parade revels in lowbrow absurdity. The pink plastic flamingo-themed parade is presided over by Don Featherstone, the real-life inventor of the pink plastic flamingo, who makes the pilgrimage north from Massachusetts every year. Following the parade is a cocktail party sponsored by the town's fictional "Yacht and Polo Club."

Despite its sometimes silly antics, Southwest Harbor remains a genuine working harbor filled with lobster boats and surrounded by boatyards. But upward pressure on real estate prices has caused some changes in recent years. As more and more "summer folks" buy homes on this side of the island, property taxes have spiraled upward, putting pressure on locals and local businesses. Hinckley Yacht Company moved its boatbuilding operations to the mainland years ago, and Ralph Stanley Boatbuilders was forced to abandon its waterfront facility in 2009. Whether or not Southwest Harbor will become completely gentrified remains to be seen, but for now it remains one of the most diverse towns on the island.

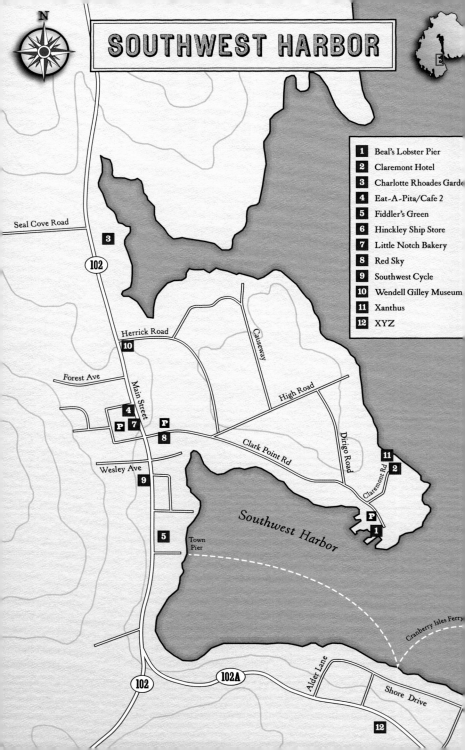

SOUTHWEST HARBOR

1	Beal's Lobster Pier
2	Claremont Hotel
3	Charlotte Rhoades Garde
4	Eat-A-Pita/Cafe 2
5	Fiddler's Green
6	Hinckley Ship Store
7	Little Notch Bakery
8	Red Sky
9	Southwest Cycle
10	Wendell Gilley Museum
11	Xanthus
12	XYZ

N

Seal Cove Road

102

Herrick Road

Forest Ave

Main Street

Causeway

High Road

Clark Point Rd

Dirigo Road

Claremont Rd

Wesley Ave

Southwest Harbor

Town Pier

Cranberry Isles Ferry

102

102A

Alder Lane

Shore Drive

★ CLAREMONT HOTEL

Perched on a hill overlooking Somes Sound, the historic Claremont Hotel offers the most elegant lodging in town. The prices are steep, but you don't have to be a guest to enjoy it. In July and August their waterfront boathouse is the best place in town for a cocktail between 5pm and 9pm, and the hotel offers a free lecture series on Thursday evenings (check the local paper for details). The hotel also features three exquisitely manicured croquet courts, and the Claremont hosts a Croquet Classic each year in early August. (800-244-5036, 22 Claremont Road)

★ ECHO LAKE

Three miles north of town is Echo Lake, the island's most popular swimming hole. At the southern end of the lake is a popular man-made beach that has changing rooms and water fountains. To get to the beach, look for the "Acadia National Park, Echo Lake Entrance" sign south of Echo Lake on Route 102. Farther north along Route 102 are Echo Lake Ledges, reached via a short, wooded path from the Acadia Mountain parking area. These small, rocky ledges are a local favorite because they're almost always less crowded than the beach.

WENDELL GILLEY MUSEUM

If you consider yourself a birder, you'll definitely want to stop at this small museum, which displays the fabulous wooden bird carvings of local legend Wendell Gilley. In addition to the permanent collection, the museum features special exhibits, bird carving demonstrations, and bird carving workshops. (4 Herrick Road, 207-244-7555)

CHARLOTTE RHOADES PARK BUTTERFLY GARDEN
This small public flower garden, expertly tended by local volunteers, is a great place to escape the crowds and enjoy the ocean views. Next to the garden there are several shaded picnic tables overlooking Norwood Cove.

CARROLL HOMESTEAD
This small house, built in 1825, offers a glimpse into the hardscrabble lives of early island settlers. On Tuesdays in July and August the park service opens the house to the public. Located off Route 102 south of Echo Lake.

MAINE GRANITE INDUSTRY HISTORICAL SOCIETY
This tiny museum, located in a lawn mower shop, has old photos and historic info, but the real draw is when the owner, Steve, uses antique hand tools to split and carve actual granite blocks. (62 Beech Hill Crossroad, 207-244-0175)

SOUTHWEST CYCLE
This is the only bike rental shop on the western side of the island, perfect if you're heading to Swans Island for the day. (207-244-5856, 370 Main St.)

Boats, Boating, & Sea Kayaking

★ DOWNEAST FRIENDSHIP SLOOP CHARTERS
One of the best sailboat tours on the island (see p.31)

DOWNEAST SAILING ADVENTURES
Choose from sailing trips on the 52-foot, two-masted schooner *Rachel B. Jackson* or the 33-foot Friendship Sloop *Surprise* (207-288-2216, www.downeastsail.com)

MASAKO QUEEN FISHING COMPANY
The 43-foot *Vagabond* offers half-day and full-day fishing trips in search of cod, mackerel, bluefish and more. Lobster traps are hauled for each passenger, and any legal sized lobsters are yours to keep. (207-244-5385, www.masakoqueen.com)

MAINE STATE SEA KAYAKING
The Quiet Side's only sea kayak outfitter offers tours of Blue Hill Bay, Western Bay and Somes Sound. The four-hour trips ($48 per person) are limited to 12 people maximum. (254 Main Street, 207-244-9500, www.mainestateseakayak.com)

HINCKLEY SHIP STORE
Even if you can't afford a Hinckley (p.261), you can load up on shirts, hats, and other Hinckley-branded gear at the official store. (130 Shore Road, 207-244-7100)

MANSELL BOAT RENTAL
Sailboat and motorboat rentals. Daily and weekly rates are available on boats from 14 to 31 feet. (207-244-5625, www.mansellboatrental.com)

Restaurants

★ RED SKY (Din: $23–29)

This is, in my opinion, the best restaurant in town, offering exquisite meals in an atmosphere the owner describes as "unstuffy elegance." Everything from the home-made pasta to the hand-cut meats is delicious, but the seafood really shines (ask for the Port Clyde Fresh Catch fish). There's also a terrific wine list and decadent desserts. (207-244-0476, 14 Clark Point Road)

★ FIDDLERS GREEN (Din: $18–28)

This casually refined restaurant has an eclectic menu that ranges from great steaks to internationally inspired seafood dishes. It also features the best beer list on the island (it even includes mead), over 100 types of wine, and 11 types of martinis. (411 Main Street, 207-244-9416)

★ XANTHUS (Din: $24–30)

Located in the historic Claremont Hotel, this is the most formal restaurant in Southwest Harbor. (For over a century they required jackets and ties, but a few years back they loosened the rules to no T-shirts and no shorts.) The setting is classy and elegant, and the food is excellent. (22 Claremont Road, 207-244-5036)

★ EAT-A-PITA/CAFE 2 (Lnch: $6–8, Din: $17-26)

Eat-A-Pita offers the best healthy sandwiches in town with pitas stuffed so full of veggies they come with a fork. At night Eat-A-Pita becomes Cafe 2, which offers creative cuisine in a laid-back atmosphere with great wines, beers and cocktails. Less expensive hamburger options are perfect if you're looking for an upscale meal but have kids in tow. (326 Main Street, 207-244-4344)

XYZ (Din: $24)

This upscale Mexican restaurant features authentic flavors from Xalapa, Yucatán and Zacatecas (XYZ). This is the best ethnic food on the island, and despite the out-of-the-way location, it's always packed. The food is tasty, the homemade margaritas are great, and the XYZ pie is legendary. (207-244-5221, 80 Seawall Road)

BEAL'S LOBSTER PIER (Lnch, Din) Market price lobster

This classic lobster shack has a rough-around-the-edges charm—picnic tables, paper plates, and salt water tanks where you can pick your own live lobster. (182 Clark Point Road, 207-244-3202)

LITTLE NOTCH BAKERY (Lnch, Din: $6-11)

This tasty bakery/sandwich shop/pizzeria offers a wide range of take-out style food, from soups and salads to pastries and paninis. (340 Main Street, 207-244-4043)

Boats & Boat Building on
MOUNT DESERT ISLAND

BOATS AND BOATBUILDING have always played a vital role on Mount Desert Island. From the Wabanaki Indians, who plied the waters in birchbark canoes, to the first settlers, who came in search of raw sailboat materials, to today's lobstermen, who captain diesel-powered craft, generations of islanders have depended on the sea as a way of life. Not surprisingly, local knowledge of boats and boatbuilding is second to none.

The most renowned MDI boatbuilder is Hinckley (www.hinckleyyachts.com), famous for its high-tech luxury yachts. Want advanced soundproofing materials built into the kevlar/carbon hull? Comes standard. Need a wine rack for slightly wider bottles from Bordeaux? They do that. What started in 1928 as a boatyard for local fishermen ultimately became a sailboat company devoted to pleasure craft. Hinckley was an early adopter of fiberglass technology in the 1950s, thrusting them to the forefront of the high-tech, luxury sailboat world. Then, in 1994, the company introduced the elegant, jet-propelled "picnic" boat (imagine a classic Maine lobsterboat redesigned for cruising and styled with lavish materials). Today picnic boats, which start around $400,000 and head well into the millions, make up the majority of their sales.

Next in line is Morris (www.morrisyachts.com), which started making high-end sailboats in 1972. Sailing remains its primary focus, and it has attracted a loyal following as a result. What's the difference between a Hinckley and a Morris? Let's just say that Martha Stewart owns a Hinckley, and Jimmy Buffett owns a Morris. Want a smaller sailboat? The Classic Boat Shop (www.classicboatshop.com) custom builds elegant, 21-foot daysailers.

Still can't find the MDI-built boat of your dreams? Ellis Boat Company (www.ellisboat.com) and John Williams (www.stanleyboats.com) offer customized boats based on traditional Downeast designs. And Wilbur Yachts (www.wilburyachts.com) builds boats any way the customer wants. Need a jacuzzi or a baby grand piano on board? Wilbur's done that.

Starting in the 1950s, most boatbuilders switched from wood to fiberglass, but one Southwest Harbor resident proudly bucked the trend. Born in 1929, Ralph Stanley (www.ralphstanleyboats.com) learned the boatbuilding craft at a time when *all* boats were made of wood. Despite the time and money savings fiberglass offered, Stanley never abandoned his love of wood. As he once told a group of local schoolchildren, "If God wanted fiberglass boats, he'd have made fiberglass trees." In 1999 Stanley was chosen as one of 12 National Heritage Fellows, and he has been named "Boatbuilder Laureate of the Maine Coast."

BASS HARBOR

Perhaps the best way to describe Bass Harbor is to describe what it's not. Located near the southwestern tip of Mount Desert Island, Bass Harbor is about as far away from Bar Harbor—both physically and metaphorically—as possible. There are no cruise ships, T-shirt shops, or tourist swarms here. Instead, Bass Harbor remains a traditional Downeast fishing village with a lobster boat-filled harbor surrounded by old wooden piers. Pickup trucks vastly outnumber SUVs, and local lawns are piled high with lobster traps and colorful buoys. On an inherently touristy island, Bass Harbor can be a breath of fresh air.

Bass Harbor is one of my favorite places on Mount Desert Island—a relaxing mix of unpretentious summer folk and hard-working locals happily removed from the crowds. And yet there's just enough to do here that you won't get bored. The area around Bass Harbor is home to Mount Desert Island's only lighthouse, two easy hiking trails, a terrific boat tour, and the island's best lobster shack. And if Bass Harbor still isn't remote enough for your taste, you can catch a ferry to Swan's Island (p.279) or Frenchboro (p.277), two small offshore islands home to traditional fishing villages.

Technically, the village of Bass Harbor lies on the eastern side of Bass Harbor, the village of Bernard lies on the western side of Bass Harbor, and both are part of the town of Tremont. If you continue north on Route 102, you'll pass the tiny communities of Goose Cove and Seal Cove before reaching Pretty Marsh.

Today Bass Harbor is home to roughly 80 lobsterboats, one of the largest fleets in Maine. But not that long ago, sardines were king. Underwood Wharf, the large brick building on the eastern side of the harbor, was once the largest sardine cannery in the state. In the 1950s there were roughly 50 sardine canneries in Maine, and they employed more people than any other industry. Back then spotter planes would find schools of herring (sardines) offshore and alert local fishermen. When herring populations dwindled in the 1960s, Underwood Wharf switched to canning blueberries, and in 1977 the cannery closed for good. Today the historic brick building has been converted into luxury condos.

Mindful that important local industries can be lost, the town has taken steps to preserve the lobster industry that still thrives here. In 2009 the family-owned Davis Wharf in Goose Cove became permanently protected for commercial fishing purposes. Today less than 20 miles of Maine's 3,000 mile coast is classified as "working waterfront" where fishermen can unload their catch. Hopefully, with proper planning, Bass Harbor can retain its traditional character for years to come.

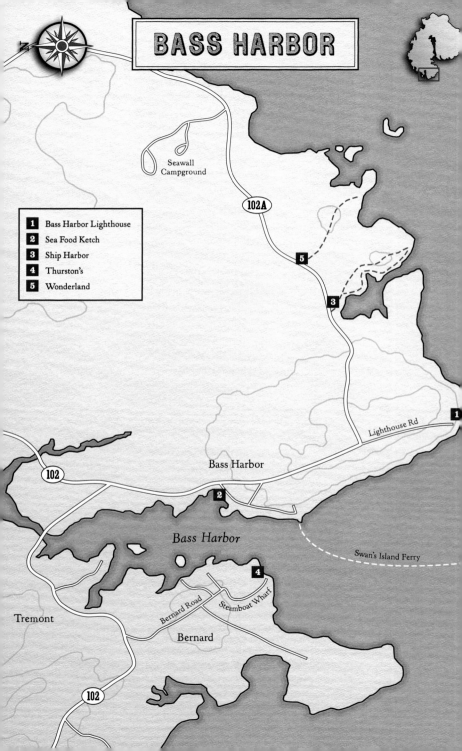

BASS HARBOR

N

1 Bass Harbor Lighthouse
2 Sea Food Ketch
3 Ship Harbor
4 Thurston's
5 Wonderland

Seawall
Campground

102A

5

3

1

Lighthouse Rd

Bass Harbor

102

2

Bass Harbor

Swan's Island Ferry

4

Bernard Road

Steamboat Wharf

Tremont

Bernard

102

★ BASS HARBOR LIGHTHOUSE

This classic Downeast lighthouse, the only one on Mount Desert Island, is Bass Harbor's must-see destination. Wooden steps lead from the parking area to the rocky shore below. Open from sunrise to sunset. (See following page.)

★ ISLAND CRUISES

This boat cruise through the islands just south of Bass Harbor is filled with fascinating info about wildlife, lobsters and local history. See page 31 for more details.

SHIP HARBOR NATURE TRAIL

This 1.3-mile round-trip trail is my favorite hike near Bass Harbor. The trail wanders through the woods and along the peaceful shores of Ship Harbor. (For decades it was thought that Ship Harbor was named for a shipwreck that occurred here around 1740, but the ship in question actually wrecked closer to Canada.) Try to arrive during low tide, when you can check out some fantastic tidepools.

WONDERLAND

This easy 1.4-mile trail heads through the woods to a nice cobblestone beach, then loops around the tip of a small, rocky peninsula. Try to visit at low tide, when several large tidepools are exposed at the edge of the peninsula.

BERNARD ROAD

This small, quiet road is home to a handful of eclectic antique shops and art galleries. Just head down the road, keep your eyes open for signs, and stop wherever strikes your fancy.

Restaurants

★ THURSTON'S (Lnch, Din: $5–11, lobsters market price)

Despite its far-flung location, Thurston's thrives because it's the best, most authentic lobster shack on the island. If you're looking for upscale dining, look elsewhere. If you're looking for unbelievably fresh lobster served on paper plates and plastic trays, welcome home! The screened-in porch offers stunning views of the harbor and the adjacent pier, where lobsterboats unload fresh lobster throughout the day. Burgers, sandwiches and tasty chowders ($5–11) are also available if you're not craving lobster (207-244-7600, Steamboat Wharf Road)

SEA FOOD KETCH (Lnch, Din: $17-24)

This waterfront restaurant combines spectacular harbor and mountain views with traditional seafood classics. The menu offers plenty of surf, some basic turf, and one of my favorite lobster rolls on the island (homemade bread makes all the difference). The outdoor patio is the real draw here, but indoor seating is also available. (207-244-7463, 47 Shore Road)

Bass Harbor Lighthouse

Since 1858 the Bass Harbor Lighthouse has been faithfully guarding the entrance to Bass Harbor and Blue Hill Bay. The beacon, originally lit by whale oil, is now powered by electricity and fully automated. All lighthouse beacons have a specific flash pattern, called a signature, which is listed on maritime charts. The red Bass Harbor beacon flashes every four seconds, and on a clear day it can be seen up to 13 miles at sea. In 1897 a 4,000-pound bronze bell was installed next to the lighthouse, but it was later replaced by offshore bell buoys. Listen closely and you'll notice that each bell buoy has a distinct pitch, which further aides in navigation on foggy days.

OFFSHORE ISLANDS

THE COAST OF MAINE is home to roughly 3,000 offshore islands—one of the highest concentrations of islands anywhere in the world. These rugged jewels—as small as a few square feet and as large as 100 square miles—add significantly to the region's mystique and provide important habitat for nesting seabirds. In addition, five offshore islands near Mount Desert Island are home to small villages with year-round populations. These islands, physically cut off from much of the modern world and largely centered around the lobster industry, are some of the most culturally unique places in America.

Today four of these islands are accessible by ferry from Mount Desert Island. Just south of Mount Desert Island lie the Cranberry Isles (p.271), five small islands named after the cranberry bogs that once flourished here. The two largest islands, Islesford and Great Cranberry Island, have year-round communities and are accessible by ferry from Northeast Harbor and Southwest Harbor. A few miles to the southwest of the Cranberry Isles lies Frenchboro (p.277) and Swan's Island (p.279), two remote islands accessible by ferry from Bass Harbor. A fifth year-round island, Isle au Haut (p.217), is accessible via the town of Stonington on the mainland.

Though largely forgotten today, Maine's offshore islands once played a starring role in the history of North America. Long before colonists landed at Jamestown, thousands of Europeans fished the rich waters of the Gulf of Maine. Arriving in the spring, they hauled up mind-boggling numbers of cod, which played a major role in providing cheap, nutritious protein to rapidly growing populations in Europe. In the late 1700s, when settlers first arrived in the region, offshore islands were considered the best places to live due to their proximity to fishing grounds and coastal shipping routes. By the late 1800s, over 300 Maine islands were populated with year-round residents. But when railroads and trucks displaced ships as the most important forms of transportation, islanders found themselves cut off from much of the modern world.

Over the past century, most of Maine's offshore islands have been abandoned as greater economic opportunities have presented themselves on the mainland. Today only 15 Maine islands have year-round populations. And though many are struggling, opportunities offered by new technologies such as the internet and wind turbines offer a glimmer of economic hope. Modern technology may have robbed the islands of their lifeblood a century ago, but it may yet breath new life into them.

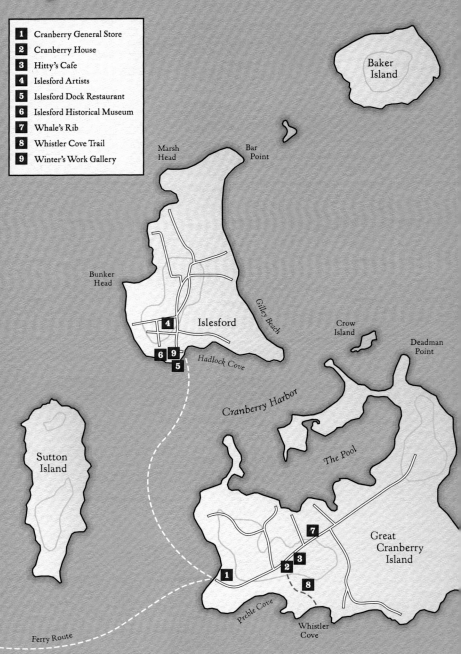

CRANBERRY ISLES

N

1 Cranberry General Store
2 Cranberry House
3 Hitty's Cafe
4 Islesford Artists
5 Islesford Dock Restaurant
6 Islesford Historical Museum
7 Whale's Rib
8 Whistler Cove Trail
9 Winter's Work Gallery

Baker
Island

Marsh
Head

Bar
Point

Bunker
Head

4 Islesford

Gilley Beach

6 9
5

Hadlock Cove

Crow
Island

Deadman
Point

Cranberry Harbor

The Pool

Sutton
Island

Great
Cranberry
Island

7

2 3

1

8

Preble Cove

Whistler
Cove

Ferry Route

CRANBERRY ISLES

THESE FIVE OFFSHORE islands—Great Cranberry, Islesford, Sutton Island, Baker Island, and Bear Island—lie just south of the eastern tip of Mount Desert Island. Originally settled in the late 1700s, the islands were named for the wild cranberries that grow here in the fall. A century ago, all five islands were occupied year-round, but today only Great Cranberry and Islesford have year-round populations. Sutton Island only has summer residents, while Baker Island and Bear Island are owned by Acadia National Park.

Both Great Cranberry and Islesford are well worth a visit. The islands' intriguing cultural mix of fishermen, artists and wealthy summer folks, combined with the spectacular views of Mount Desert Island, makes for a truly unique day trip. Far removed from the traffic and crowds on the mainland, the pace of island life is distinctly relaxed. Don't be surprised if nearly everyone you encounter waves at you and says "Hi."

At their peak nearly 100 years ago, both Great Cranberry and Islesford had booming shipyards, multiple schools and vibrant fishing fleets. But over the past century, as populations dwindled, many of the old institutions have vanished. The schoolhouse on Great Cranberry, though technically active, has no students, and the schoolhouse on Little Cranberry has fewer than a dozen students. Today the median age on the Cranberry Isles is 45, and fewer than 30 people are younger than 20. The economic pulse of the islands still revolves around the sea with boatbuilding and fishing as the primary occupations.

For more on the Cranberry Isles, visit www.cranberryisles.com

Getting to the Cranberry Isles

Beal & Bunker - This official mailboat to the Cranberry Isles, in service since 1950, departs year-round from Northeast Harbor. (207-244-3575)

Cranberry Cove Ferry - From May to October, the *Island Queen* offers daily shuttles between Southwest Harbor and the Cranberry Isles. (207-244-5882)

Sea Princess - Departing daily from Northeast Harbor, this tourboat offers nature trips and an Islesford Historical Cruise. (207-276-5352)

The Delight - This 6-person water taxi offers service to the Cranberry Isles from Northeast Harbor, Seal Harbor or Southwest Harbor. You can also book private sunset cruises to the Islesford Dock Restaurant. (207-244-5724)

Islesford

Islesford, aka "Little Cranberry Island," is the most populated of the Cranberry Isles with 200 plus summer residents and 70 year-round residents. It's also the most tourist-friendly island due to its dockside restaurant, historical museum, and numerous art galleries. You can bring a bike, but it's very easy to walk around Islesford, which only has a handful of paved roads. After exploring Islesford, you can check out the economic heart of the Cranberry Islands at the Islesford Lobster Co-op, located next to the town pier. Throughout the day, lobsterman unload their catch and buy bait at the Co-op. If you're planning a trip to Islesford, be sure to check out the island's official website: www.islesford.com

★ ISLESFORD HISTORICAL MUSEUM

This small museum, founded in 1919 and currently operated by Acadia National Park, features exhibits and artifacts relating to early settler's lives on the Cranberry Isles. The museum is open from 9:30am–12:00 and 12:30pm–3:30pm, mid-June through September.

★ ISLESFORD DOCK RESTAURANT (Lnch, Din) Entrees $9-23

This waterfront restaurant, perched on a 200-year-old coal dock overlooking the harbor, offers great food and stunning views of Mount Desert Island. The menu offers plenty of fresh seafood, plus burgers and interesting entrees like Korean Pork Ssam. Open mid-June to early-Sept. No lunch on Mondays. *The Delight* (p.271) offers sunset dinner cruises to the restaurant from Northeast Harbor.

★ ART GALLERIES

A short stroll up the road from the dock takes you to **Islesford Artists** (Mosswood Road, www.islesfordartists.com), the most impressive gallery on the island. The gallery, founded by lobsterman/artist Dan Fernald showcases the work of artists from Islesford and other Maine islands. On the Islesford Dock you'll find **Islesford Pottery**, which offers plenty of pottery, jewelry and homemade fudge. **Winter's Work** (www.winterswork.com), also on the Islesford Dock, is a small gallery with an eclectic collection. And finally, behind the Islesford Market you'll find Island Girl Seaglass, which features folksy seaglass jewelry.

THE ALLEYWAY LUNCH TRUCK

When the Islesford Market closed in 2008, Cari Alley, the wife of a local lobsterman, bought a lunch truck, parked it near the pier, and began selling snacks, sandwiches, Islesford's famous white gingerbread, and one of the region's most affordable lobster rolls (she buys the lobsters directly from her husband).

JOY OF KAYAKING

Local postmaster Joy Sprague rents single and double sea kayaks. She only has a few kayaks, so it's best to call ahead for reservations (207-244-4309)

Great Cranberry Island

At 1,000 acres, Great Cranberry is the largest of the Cranberry Isles, but its year-round population is just 40 people. With the arrival of the summer folks, however, the island's population swells to about 250. It's entirely possible to explore the island on foot, but a bike will certainly come in handy. Also check the bulletin board in the shack on the pier for up-to-date info on island happenings.

CRANBERRY GENERAL STORE

Not far from the town dock is this small, but well-supplied market, which sells everything from food to beer to cleaning supplies. Inside the market you'll find the Seawich Cafe, which sells basic sandwiches.

CRANBERRY HOUSE

This recently restored house, originally built in the early 1900s, is home to the Great Cranberry Island Historical Society's Preble-Marr Museum, which features displays on the history of Great Cranberry Island. In addition to displays on ship-building and the island's early settlers, there's a section devoted to Cranberry Isles summer resident Rachel Field, who wrote the popular children's book "Hitty: Her First Hundred Years." Above the museum is the Art Center, a gathering place for classes, movies and lectures.

WHISTLER COVE TRAIL

This easy, well-marked trail leads to a beautiful cobblestone beach at Whistler Cove. The trail, which takes 30–40 minutes round-trip, starts behind Cranberry House, and heads through a mossy forest. Along the way you'll pass over many narrow wooden planks placed over the boggy terrain.

HITTY'S CAFE

This small cafe, located in Cranberry House, serves soups, sandwiches, salads and homemade baked goods.

WHALE'S RIB

This small gift shop and gallery, run by local resident Polly Bunker, sells a variety of local creations.

Baker Island

Baker Island, the most remote of the Cranberry Islands, was settled roughly two hundred years ago by William and Hannah Gilley. The Gilleys and their 12 children raised cows, chickens and roughly 50 sheep on the 123-acre island. In 1828 a 26-foot lighthouse was built on Baker Island, and in 1855 the original lighthouse was replaced with the current 43-foot tall tower. Today the island is owned by Acadia National Park. Ranger-guided boat tours of Baker Island are offered on the *Miss Samantha* (p.230).

Islesford & Mount Desert Island

Frenchboro

ISLANDS SOUTH OF BASS HARBOR

Frenchboro

This 1,500-acre island, home to a year-round population of roughly 40 people, is officially called Long Island. But because there are several Long Islands in Maine, locals call it Frenchboro—the name of the island's one tiny village. The island was first settled in 1813, and in 1910 the population peaked at 197. Since then a steady stream of islanders has left for the mainland, and today the local economy revolves entirely around lobsters and lobstering. Despite the small population, nearly a dozen children attend K-7 in the island's one-room schoolhouse, and in 2009 the villagers were featured on an episode of *Oprah* entitled "Life in Isolated Communities."

Frenchboro is famous for its annual Lobster Festival, held the second Saturday of August. The festival is the biggest party of the year, attracting over 500 people who arrive by lobster boat, private yacht or via a special ferry that departs from Bass Harbor in the morning. If you miss the festival, you can still enjoy fresh lobster at Lunt's Dockside Deli (207-334-2922) in July and August. Unless you have your own boat, the best way to visit Frenchboro is with Island Cruises (p.31), which offers day trips to Frenchboro from Bass Harbor. For more information about Frenchboro, check out www.frenchboroonline.com

Placentia

In 1948 Arthur and Nancy Kellam purchased this 500-acre island for $10,000, and for the next 35 years they lived there year-round in near total seclusion. There was no running water or electricity. They chopped their own wood and grew their own vegetables. And when they needed supplies such as kerosene or batteries, they rowed several miles to the mainland to purchase them. Although the Kellams did not welcome visitors to their island, a handful of locals knew of their existence. One was David Rockefeller, who accidentally met them while island shopping in the 1960s. "I felt that they had been burned by life, and the world, that they had to get away and be by themselves," Rockefeller told a reporter in 2003. Some believed that Arthur, a former aviation engineer, had worked on the Manhattan Project. Others maintained they were simply back-to-the-landers seeking intellectual peace in the wilderness. According to Nancy Kellam's journal describing their move to the island, "At 3 o'clock on the 23rd of May, Art cashed his last salary check, then we made a little round of calls, paying respects to civilization before turning our backs on it ... we hoped to build a simple house and a simple life, to learn to appreciate fundamental things." In 1985 Arthur died of pneumonia and his ashes were spread on the island. After spending three summers and one winter on Placentia by herself, Nancy moved to Bass Harbor. Following her death in 2001, Placentia was donated to the Nature Conservancy.

SWAN'S ISLAND

LYING SIX MILES southwest of Mount Desert Island, Swan's Island features 7,000 acres of classic coastal scenery and one of the prettiest harbors in Maine. Home to roughly 350 year-round residents, visiting Swan's Island feels a bit like stepping back in time. Other than satellite TV and the internet, little has changed here over the past several decades, and the island's tight-knit fishing community continues to live a life that revolves entirely around the sea. If you're looking for the salt of the earth, it doesn't get much saltier than Swan's Island.

Swan's Island also boasts one of the most colorful histories of any Maine island. When French explorer Samuel Champlain first set eyes on the island in 1604, he named it *Brûlé Côté*, "Burnt Coast"—presumably because wildfires had recently burned the island. Over the years, Brule Cote's pronunciation and spelling was twisted and mangled to "Burnt Coat," which is now the official name of Swan's Island's most famous harbor. Even today, Swan's Island continues to engage in linguistic lawlessness. Since 1986 island residents have made a deliberate attempt to restore the historically accurate apostrophe to Swan's Island—in defiance of nautical charts and the U.S. Postal Service.

Swan's Island's first white settler was Thomas Kench, who fled here after going AWOL during the Revolutionary War. For over a decade Kench lived on the island as a hermit. Then one morning he awoke to find settlers arriving by boat. He was horrified to learn that the island had been purchased by his former Revolutionary War commander: Colonel James Swan. Apparently tensions between Swan and Kench had eased considerably by then, for Kench lived on the island an additional 10 years before moving to the mainland.

To populate his new island, Colonel Swan offered 100 acres to any homesteader who promised to stay at least seven years. The first man to accept this offer was David Smith, who arrived here from New Hampshire in 1791. Over the course of his life, Smith fathered 27 children by three wives, earning him the local nickname "King David." (Today many Swan's Island residents can still trace their family lineage back to King David.)

At its peak in the late 1800s, Swan's Island boasted a population of over 700 and its fishermen were consistently ranked first or second in Maine in terms of annual catch. During the 1900s, when gas-powered engines made offshore fishing from the mainland possible, the island lost over half of its year-round population.

Today Swan's Island is accessible via a 30-minute ferry that departs from Bass Harbor several times daily. The ferry is operated by the Maine State Ferry Service, which publishes ferry schedules online, but it's always best to call and confirm departure times (207-244-3254). Ferry tickets are available inside the building next to the ferry ramp in Bass Harbor. Swan's Island's 27 miles of paved, uncrowded roads are perfect for bikes, which can be rented in Southwest Harbor (p.258).

For more on Swan's Island, check out www.swansisland.org

SWAN'S ISLAND

1 Boat House Restaurant
2 Carrying Place Market
3 Fine Sand Beach
4 Granite Quarry
5 Hockamock Head Lighthouse
6 Island Bake Shoppe
7 Lobster & Marine Museum
8 Mill Pond Park
9 Saturn Press

The Sisters

Red Point

Goose Pond

North Point

Bass Harbor Ferry

Mackerel Cove

Atlantic Village

4

8

Burnt Coat Harbor

1

5

2

Toothacher Cove

Buckle Harbor

3

Irish Point

Seal Cove

Swans Island Head

Hat Island

West Point

★ HOCKAMOCK HEAD LIGHTHOUSE

Originally built in 1872 and automated in 1975, this classic square lighthouse stands guard over the entrance to Burnt Coat Harbor. Perched at the tip of a narrow peninsula, it boasts tremendous views of both the harbor and the Gulf of Maine.

★ FINE SAND BEACH

This small, gorgeous beach could be my favorite beach in Maine. It's certainly the loneliest. On a hot summer day, there's no better place to plop down, soak in the sun, and watch the lobstermen haul traps in Toothacher Cove. The beach is accessible via a short hiking trail through the woods.

MILL POND PARK

This lovely park, located just down the hill from the Mill Pond Health Center, offers picnic tables, grill, and terrific views of Burnt Coat Harbor.

GRANITE QUARRY

The island's old granite quarry is now used as a swimming hole. Even if you don't go swimming, the road to the quarry offers classic views of the harbor, the lighthouse, and piers full of lobster traps and colorful buoys.

SATURN PRESS

Since 1986 this high-end print shop has been making stationary and greeting cards using antique letterpresses. Informal tours are given, and you can even watch the presses running through windows in the gift shop. Open Mon-Fri, 9am–5pm. (463 Atlantic Road, 207-526-4001)

LOBSTER & MARINE MUSEUM

This small museum, located in a grey shingle house about 100 yards northeast of the ferry terminal, offers several rooms full of fishing and lobstering artifacts. There are old photos, antique fishing gear, boat models, and the shell of a giant lobster. (207-526-4423)

ISLAND BAKE SHOPPE

This small restaurant, located just down the road from the ferry terminal, serves breakfast and lunch. Options include sandwiches, salads, chowder, and homemade baked goods. (73 Ferry Terminal Road, 207-526-4123)

CARRYING PLACE MARKET & TAKE-OUT

This small market sells cold drinks, snacks, and canned goods. Next door, a take-out lunch truck sells burgers, hot dogs, pizza and subs. (207-526-4043)

BOAT HOUSE RESTAURANT AND GIFT SHOP

This ramshackle restaurant, perched above Burnt Coat Harbor, offers sandwiches, burgers, and ice cream. (207-526-4201)

the remarkable life of
JAMES SWAN

The story of James Swan, the first owner of Swan's Island, is one of the most colorful tales in American History. In 1675, when Swan was just 11 years old, he arrived in America from Scotland. By age 17 the ambitious self-taught youngster had written a book arguing against the Slave Trade, making him one of America's earliest Abolitionists. Later he joined the Sons of Liberty, participated in the Boston Tea Party, and fought at Bunker Hill (where he was wounded twice). Following the war, he was elected to the Massachusetts State Legislature. Shortly after his election, he inherited a large fortune from a wealthy Scotsman who, though not related to Swan, admired Swan's ambition. Swan used the money to purchase and sell confiscated Tory property, multiplying his inheritance several times over.

Armed with newfound wealth, Swan led an increasingly flamboyant lifestyle. He speculated in risky investments, fought (and won) a duel, and boasted of owning the most luxurious horse-drawn carriage in America. In 1786 Swan purchased Swan's Island and most of the small islands surrounding it. He referred to this property as his "Island Empire" and built a grand mansion on Swan's Island where he entertained guests in lavish style. But just one year after purchasing Swan's Island, many of his risky investments turned sour. To make up for his losses, he invested in even riskier ventures. When trace amounts of gold were discovered on Swan's Island, Swan spent huge sums of money establishing a full scale mining operation. Three years later, the mining operation had produced enough gold to make "one good sized wedding ring."

As Swan's debts compounded, he was forced to flee to Paris to escape his creditors and try to rebuild his fortune. Using aristocratic connections, Swan landed several lucrative contracts with the French Army, but the contracts fell apart with the onset of the French Revolution. Although Swan escaped the guillotine, he was later arrested by French authorities for an alleged debt of two million francs. Although Swan had the money, he insisted that he did not owe it and refused to pay—a noble stance that landed him in prison for the next 22 years. While incarcerated, Swan paid off many of the debts of his fellow inmates, but he refused to even speak with the man who claimed he was owed two million francs.

By the time Swan was finally released from French prison, he was 76 years old. His wife and most of his friends had passed away. Having nowhere to go, Swan returned to prison and pleaded to become an inmate again. His offer was refused. Three years later, Swan died alone on a Paris street.

Swan's Island

The Best of the Best

www.jameskaiser.com